SHARING NATURE
With CHILDREN

THE CLASSIC PARENTS' & TEACHERS' NATURE AWARENESS GUIDEBOOK

by Joseph Cornell

Sharing Nature Series, Volume One

Second Edition 🐾 Revised and Expanded

TO
Those who experience
nature's inspiring, transforming
moments, and who desire to share with others
their love for the natural world.

AND
S.K., who by simply living his life,
has given me a greater understanding of my own.

Copyright © 1998 Joseph Cornell

Publisher's Cataloging-in-Publication (Provided by Quality Books, Inc.)

Cornell, Joseph Bharat
    Sharing nature with children: the classic parents' and teachers' nature awareness guidebook / by Joseph Cornell. – 2nd ed.
    p. cm.
ISBN: 1-883220-73-4
Includes indexes

1. Nature study. 2. Natural history—Study and teaching. 3. Games in ecology education. 4. Outdoor games. I Title.

QH53.C77 1998   508'.071
QBI97-41066

Published by DAWN Publications
14618 Tyler Foote Road
Nevada City, CA 95959
(530) 478-7540

10 9 8 7 6 5 4 3 2 1
Second Edition
Printed in Canada
on recycled paper with vegetable based ink.

Contents

6

Foreword

I FIRST MET Joseph Cornell at a train station in Dayton,
Ohio. He had just arrived from California to partici-
pate in a thirteen-week Naturalist Training Program at
the National Audubon Society's Aullwood Center. As I
approached the station at 2:00 A.M., I spotted Joseph lying
on his back on a small triangular piece of lawn in front of the
terminal, resting and meditating on the intoxicating beauty
of the night sky. As I approached, he jumped to his feet and
greeted me with, as I was to learn, typical enthusiasm. This
was the beginning of an exciting, rewarding relationship.

The Aullwood staff were taken by Joseph's naturalness
and love for the Earth. When he was in the outdoors, it was
obvious that Joseph was in his element: he spoke to the trees,
touched them with love—and, yes, even embraced them. He
had a childlike quality, and it always seemed that to him the
Earth was a place of beauty and mystery. He loved to work
with children, and his uninhibited joyfulness allowed children to be themselves around him: to play Indians in the
tall prairie grass, to climb a tree, to do all those things children love doing. And while he played with them, Joseph always promoted perception and sensitivity toward the Earth.
While at Aullwood, he wrote a short paper on environmental games, which we still use as a handout for teachers and
youth leaders; and this book is a natural extension of that
earlier effort.

In today's world of overpopulation and high consump-
tion, it is essential that we make an effort to keep people in
touch with the Earth: its natural rhythms, the changing

seasons, its beauty and mystery. In fact, nothing will suffice, short of teaching people to love.

Henry David Thoreau wrote: "The Earth is more to be admired than to be used." And in her book, *The Sense of Wonder,* Rachel Carson claimed that, when introducing a child to the excitement of the natural world, "It is not half so important to *know* as to *feel.*" It is in this spirit that Joseph has written his book—as an aid to youth leaders in helping children to become more aware of the world around them, and to help them to know the deep personal satisfaction of being in touch with the Earth.

Paul E. Knoop, Jr.
Program Director (retired)
Aullwood National Audubon Center and Farm

Preface to the First Edition

THE UNUTTERABLE BEAUTY of a blossom. The grace of a high-flying bird. The roar of wind in the trees: At one time or another in our lives, nature touches you ... and me ... and all of us in some personal, special way. Her immense mystery opens to us a little of its stunning purity, reminding us of a Life that is greater than the little affairs of man.

I have never underestimated the value of such moments of touching and entering into nature. I have seen through my own experience and that of many others, that we can nourish that deeper awareness until it becomes a true and vital understanding of our place in this world

I collected and developed the games in this book during years of working with children as a nature-awareness instructor. I wanted to help children to have the high inspirations that nature offers; because nature is our Mother, and her lessons are especially valuable for the growing child. And so that is what this book is all about: using nature to stimulate joyful, enlightening insights and experiences—for ourselves, as well as for our children and child-friends.

Some people have scientific, logical minds, while others are more sensitively attuned to beauty and harmony; and still others are moved most deeply by the eternal philosophical truths. The 50 games presented in this book will open up nature to children—and adults—of all temperaments. Each of the games creates a situation, or an experience, in which nature is the teacher. Each game is a mouth through which nature speaks—sometimes in the language of the scientist, sometimes in that of the artist or mystic.

The first group of games brings us into harmony with our natural surroundings on the physical and emotional level.

Later on there are games that create a quiet, contemplative mood. (Don't think for a minute that the "quiet" games are boring; I've seen players experience such calm, intense alertness that their memories of the games stayed with them for years, giving fresh inspiration every time those memories were brought to mind.)

Some of the games give us an inside view of the way nature works—the principles of ecological systems, for example—but not in a dull, textbook way. While we play the games, we act out dynamically, and feel directly, the natural cycles and processes. Children understand and remember concepts best when they learn from direct personal experience.

Still other games tune our finer feelings to special qualities of nature—her peace and beauty; her energy and grandeur; her mystery and wonder. We commune with nature directly by touch, smell, taste, sight, and sound.

Some of the games are purely fun. The natural exuberance of childhood is in its element in the woods or in tall grass, or under a starlit summer sky. As adults, we cherish our memories of such childhood scenes, because they touch something deep inside us.

I happily offer these nature-awareness games to you and your child-friends. Use them sensitively and with joy and you're sure to experience a beautiful new attunement and exchange of energy with nature's intelligence and goodness.

Joseph Cornell
Nevada City, California
November, 1978

Preface to the Second Edition

WHEN I BEGAN as a teaching naturalist in the 1970s, I remember discovering how dynamic and effective nature activities can be. The experiences I had while teaching nature games thrilled me because I saw how they enabled people to have their own direct experience of nature.

I wrote *Sharing Nature with Children* because I passionately wanted others to know about these wonderful games, and this exciting way of teaching. Since the book's publication in 1979, it's been a joy to see thousands of people embrace its activities and philosophy with enthusiasm equal to my own.

Since first describing the activities twenty years ago, I've learned a lot from the feedback I've received and from teaching the activities in a wide variety of settings. This expanded 20th anniversary edition gives me the opportunity to add eight new activities and rewrite and add refinements to 20 of the 42 original ones.

Today, parents and teachers use *Sharing Nature with Children* in virtually every country in the world. It's been published in over 15 languages, and there are Sharing Nature groups in Japan, Brazil, Taiwan, Germany, and England. A 6,000-member organization in Japan, comprised of university professors, teachers, and naturalists, furthers the Sharing Nature philosophy and methods. Sharing Nature Worldwide was established in 1997 to help bring together people in all lands.

People frequently ask me if I've had to adapt the Sharing Nature games for foreign cultures. Actually, I've found that very little adaptation is required. When I first taught Sharing Nature workshops in Japan in 1986, people there said the activities were "very Japanese." And in Greece last year I was told, "They're very Greek."

What makes the Sharing Nature activities so popular? I believe it's because in addition to teaching ecology creatively, these games help people experience a profound sense of joy, serenity, and belonging to the natural world.

I wish you many beautiful and inspiring moments as you play these games with your friends young and old.

Joseph Cornell
Nevada City, California
February, 1998

How to Be
An Effective
Nature Guide

(A Few Suggestions for Good Teaching)

BEFORE WE BEGIN exploring nature with children, let's think for a moment about our role as teacher/guides. What are the basic rules for giving children—and ourselves—a joyous, rewarding good time?

I would like to share with you five tenets of outdoor teaching that have helped me work with children's lively energies—channeling them away from mischief, and toward more constructive, and ultimately satisfying, pursuits. Underlying these principles are basic attitudes of respect for children and reverence for nature—attitudes to which they will surely respond.

1. Teach less, and share more. Besides telling children the bare facts of nature ("This is a mountain hemlock tree."), I like to tell them about my inner feelings in the presence of that hemlock tree. I tell them about my awe and respect for the way a hemlock can survive in sub-alpine conditions—where water is scarce in summer, and mostly frozen in winter; where harsh winter winds twist and bend and scour its branches. And I tell them I always wonder how the roots of the hemlock ever manage to find enough nutrients to survive, in these solid-rock crevices.

Children respond to my observations much more freely than they respond to textbook explanations. Take the case of a hemlock tree that grew near a camp where I worked. This particular hemlock sits between two huge boulders, so it has had to send its roots down twenty-five feet to reach the rocky soil below. At the time, it was at least two hundred years old, and only eight feet tall. The children would frequently make a detour on their hikes just to empty their canteens by its roots. Several of them returned to the camp year after year, watching the tree's stubborn struggle for life in its harsh environment. In fact, as soon as they arrived at camp, they would run out to see how it had fared through the dry autumn and cold winter. Their loving concern awakened in me an even deeper respect for the mountain hemlock.

I believe it is important for an adult to share his inner self with the child. Only by sharing our deeper thoughts and feelings do we communicate to, and inspire in others, a love and respect for the Earth. When we share our own ideas and feelings, it encourages a child to explore, respectfully, his own feelings and perceptions. A wonderful mutual trust and friendship develops between the adult and the child.

2. *Be receptive.* Receptivity means listening, and being aware. It is one of the most richly rewarding attitudes you can cultivate while working with children. The outdoors brings out a spontaneous enthusiasm in the child that you can skillfully direct toward learning.

Be sensitive: every question, every comment, every joyful exclamation is an opportunity to communicate. Respond to the child's present mood and feelings. Expand your child's interests by teaching along the grain of his own curiosity. When you respect his thoughts, you'll find your time with him flowing easily and happily.

Be alert also to what nature is doing around you at the present moment. Something exciting or interesting is almost always happening. Your lesson plan will be written for you minute by minute if you tune in with sensitive attention.

3. *Focus the child's attention without delay.* Set the tone of the outing right at the start. Involve everyone as much as you can, by asking questions and pointing out interesting sights and sounds. Some children are not used to watching nature closely, so find things that interest them, and lead them bit by bit into the spirit of keen observation. Let them feel that their findings are interesting to you, too.

4. *Look and experience first; talk later.* At times nature's spectacles will seize the child in rapt attention: a newly-emerged dragonfly pumping blood into tender unfolding wings, a lone deer grazing in a forest clearing. But even if those special sights are lacking, the child can have an experience of wonder by just watching quiet ordinary things with close attention. Children

have a marvelous capacity for absorbing themselves in whatever they're looking at. They will gain a far better understanding of things outside themselves by becoming one with them than from second-hand talk. Children seldom forget a direct experience.

Don't feel badly about not knowing names. The names of plants and animals are only superficial labels for what those things really *are*. Just as your own essence isn't captured by your name, or even by your physical and personality traits, there is also much more to an oak tree, for example, than a name and a list of facts about it. You can gain a deeper appreciation of an oak tree by watching how the tree's mood shifts with changes in lighting at different times of day. Observe the tree from unusual perspectives. Feel and smell its bark and leaves. Quietly sit on or under its branches, and be aware of all the forms of life that live in and around the tree and depend on it.

Look. Ask questions. Guess. Have fun! As your children begin to develop an attunement with nature, your relationship with them will evolve from one of teacher and fellow-student to one of fellow-adventurer.

5. *A sense of joy should permeate the experience,* whether in the form of gaiety or calm attentiveness. Children are naturally drawn to learning if you can keep the spirit of the occasion happy and enthusiastic. Remember that your own enthusiasm is contagious, and that it is perhaps your greatest asset as a teacher.

Choosing the Right Game for the Time and Place

THE NATURE GAMES in this book will teach children many kinds of lessons—some obvious, some quite subtle. You may want to use certain games because of the concepts they teach, or because of the personal qualities they teach. You can also choose games to complement the mood of your group, or to create a desirable change in attitude or energy. To make it easy for you to tell quickly what each game is like, I have included with each activity a quick-reference list, such as the following:

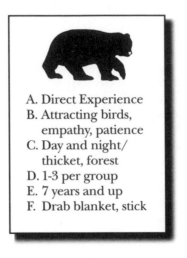

A. Direct Experience
B. Attracting birds,
   empathy, patience
C. Day and night/
   thicket, forest
D. 1-3 per group
E. 7 years and up
F. Drab blanket, stick

Each line or symbol has the following meaning.

Symbol. Basic mood of each game, as indicated by one of four animal symbols:

Awaken Enthusiasm   *Energetic/Playful*
The otter spends his days frolicking; the only animal that plays (constantly!) throughout adult life, he is nature's embodiment of exuberant fun.

Focus Attention   *Attentive/Observational*
The crow is an extremely alert and intelligent rascal, who's likely to be found keenly observing anything that's going on.

Direct Experience   *Calm/Experiential*
Bears are very curious, and lead solitary, quiet lives. Their temperament makes them a perfect symbol for deeply experiencing nature.

Share Inspiration   *Reflective/Sharing*
Dolphins are gregarious and altruistic creatures. They cooperate and care for one another, and they also appear to be conscious of other forms of life. Dolphins beautifully express the qualities of sharing and altruism.

A. The concepts, attitudes and qualities it teaches
B. When and where to play
C. Number of players needed
D. Best age range
E. Special materials needed, if any

It is very effective to use the games sequentially. For example, you'll probably want to play the fun and exciting Otter games first in order to awaken your group's enthusiasm. Then play the Crow games to focus everyone's attention. Once the children are attentive, they can better appreciate the more sensitive and experiential Bear games. The Dolphin games make for a perfect ending because they encourage everyone to share the inspiration they are feeling.

At the end of the book, you will find all the games indexed in four ways: (1) according to the attitudes and qualities they encourage in children; (2) according to the concepts they teach; (3) according to the environment in which they can best be used; and (4) according to the mood they express. I hope that this system will enable you to make the best, most creative use of these games and activities.

CLOSE-UP WITH NATURE

In Ohio many years ago, a naturalist at an outdoor education camp led a group of children on a very special hike. I was a participant rather than a leader that day, and I still enjoy my memories of the outing. Our guide created dramatic, contrasting experiences for us that ensured that all of us would have deep, new, personal contacts with the natural world.

Most of the children had never been in an evergreen forest in their lives, and we were going to one of the few pine forests in southern Ohio. (This stand of pines was planted many years ago as part of an arboretum, a place where trees are scientifically studied.) The children were excited, and our naturalist-guide channeled their high energy skillfully to create a moving experience of the forest.

She first took us to a Christmas-tree farm, where she announced with a flourishing sweep of an arm and a twinkle in her eye, "This is the pine forest." Groans and disappointed *shuffling of feet—the trees were barely taller than the children.*

She then blindfolded all of us and led us through a sunny deciduous forest. Pretty soon we heard a stream and she said, "There's a narrow bridge here, so you'll have to cross one at a time." The first child started across, then shrieked with nervous laughter. The rest of us waited uneasily, not knowing what was ahead.

My turn came and I groped my way forward, taking a first cautious step onto the bridge. Aha! No wonder there were squeals—the bridge swayed dizzily from side to side, and bounced up and down at the same time. Between the creaks and groans of ropes and wood, I heard water rushing along far below. At the other side I was greeted by a flutter of small hands; the naturalist had let the children take off their blindfolds to watch me cross. I now removed my own blindfold and saw a safely-built suspension bridge, its handrails polished from much use.

We replaced our blindfolds and struck out on the trail again. After awhile the sound of our footsteps changed; we heard no more crackling leaves, only a soft, muffled crunching as we walked. Then there was a dark shadow all around us and we sensed a deep quiet—fewer bird sounds, and no rustling of leaves in the wind. A child broke the silence: "Where are we?"

The naturalist said, "Lie down on your backs and try to feel what is special about this place."

We lay for a long time experiencing the deep, restful quiet. Finally, the naturalist told us to take off our blindfolds. Shooting skyward were countless magnificent pine trees. My spirits rose with them, and I was overwhelmed with admiration and awe—I had never seen a forest this way before. The children were completely stunned. Finally, we sat up and looked around at each other, quietly sharing our amazement. On our own we wandered through the forest, touching the trees and gazing up into the forest cathedral.

It takes a happy combination of setting and receptivity to have a really deep experience like this. That's what the games in this chapter are for: to bring us that fresh and mysterious contact with other members of the natural world.

A. Direct Experience
B. Aesthetic appreciation, visual awareness
C. Day/forest floor
D. 1 or more
E. 7 years and up
F. None

THE FOREST looks fresh and exciting, when you see it from a brand-new angle. In this game, the children lie still on the forest floor, absorbed in watching and listening to swaying trees, fluttering birds, and the rushing wind. Through holes in its leafy ceiling, silent clouds peek into the children's woodsy room. Animals may come very close because the children are quiet and hidden.

Have everyone lie down and begin thinking of himself as part of the Earth, looking skyward. Cover each child's body with leaves, sticks and pine needles—clear up to the sides of his head. Leave only the face exposed, and use enough leaves and sticks to give him a feeling of being down inside the Earth. Now place leaves (pine needles work best) over the children's faces, patchwork-fashion. Make sure the leaves are free of dirt, and tell the children to close their eyes as you arrange this final bit of covering.

Tell the children you'll give a signal when it's time to come back; this will help them stay under the leaves longer without getting restless. You should give the signal before they become restless. Surprisingly, I've found that twenty minutes is usually not too long.

In a large group, work quickly and have the children help bury each other. Work in one direction, away from those covered first. Then when the first-covered emerge, you can steer them away from the others who are still enjoying the forest quiet. Any individuals or pairs who are likely to talk and disturb those around them can be buried some distance away from the others.

Children will be much more agreeable to the idea of being covered with soil and leaves if they've been digging or crawling on the forest floor just before the game begins. It's important also to say something in advance about the bugs that may crawl over them. Play this down! You may want to let the children first handle various bugs, allowing the bugs to crawl over them. This is often a lot of fun— the children lose their early-learned prejudices against insects, and begin to appreciate these fascinating little creatures. Encourage them to stay calm while lying under the leaves and being crawled upon; ask them just to feel what the bug is doing, so that they can tell the others about it afterwards.

Earth Windows gives an experience of the forest through the forest's own eyes.

Earth Windows

A. Direct Experience
B. Empathy, tree
   physiology
C. Day/forest
D. 1 or more
E. 4 years and up
F. Stethoscope

A

TREE is a living creature.
It eats, rests, breathes and circulates its "blood" much as we do. The heartbeat of a tree is a wonderful crackling, gurgling flow of life. The best time to hear the forest heartbeat is in early spring, when the trees send first surges of sap upward to their branches, preparing them for another season of growth.

Choose a tree that is at least six inches in diameter and has thin bark. Deciduous trees are generally better for listening to than conifers, and certain individuals of a species may have a louder heartbeat than others. Press a stethoscope firmly against the tree, keeping it motionless so as not to make interfering noises. You may have to try several different places on the tree trunk before you find a good listening spot.

Children will want to hear their own heartbeat. Listen also to the heartbeats of mammals and birds—the variety in sounds and rhythms is fascinating.

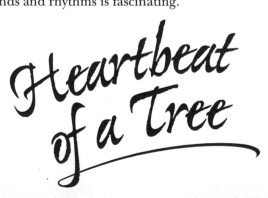

Heartbeat of a Tree

An Introduction to the Blind Activities

THE GAMES in this section stimulate children's imaginations as perhaps no other games in this book can.

Blindfolded activities dislodge our thoughts from self-preoccupation, and free our awareness to embrace more of the world around us. Vision is the sense we depend on most. Deprived of sight, we must fall back on our less-used senses of hearing, touch and smell. Our attention is powerfully focused on these senses, and our perceptions through them are intensified. The babbling of our minds slows down, overwhelmed by the information that our fully-awake senses are giving us.

I vividly remember my first blindfolded experience. I was led down a path to a creek, which I entered up to my knees, splashing around and feeling the current. My guide asked me if I'd like to float downstream. Well, in we went! At first we floated cautiously, but soon I was able to relax and give myself to the current, drifting along wherever it led. I was delighted by the crosscurrents that turned and twisted my body, while gurglings, roarings, swishings and bubblings composed the most wonderful music. I had never known a creek to be such a marvelous thing!

(Caution: Unless you and your guide are familiar with the particular stream, and water safety procedures, it would be best to start your blind experiences with one of the activities in this chapter.)

A. Direct Experience
B. Sensory awareness, trust
C. Day/anywhere
D. 2 or more
E. 7 years and up
F. Blindfolds

Blind Walk

I T'S VERY SIMPLE to organize and lead a blind walk. Form pairs, with mixed adults and children, or children together, if they're mature enough. Each pair decides who'll be the leader first, and who'll be blindfolded. The leader guides his partner along any route that looks attractive—being very careful to watch for logs, low branches, and so on. The leader also guides his blind partner's hands to interesting objects, and brings him within range of interesting sounds and smells. Remember to demonstrate how to lead one's partner safely, and to remind the leaders that *they* are the eyes for their blindfolded partners.

When people try something new, they're often nervous and cover it up by joking and laughing. Since covering one's eyes is a novel experience for many children, it's helpful to play the following game before a **Blind Walk**. *Ask everyone to sit in a circle and close their eyes. Tell them that you are going to pass an object around the circle and each person is to use his sense of smell, touch, and possibly hearing to discover something new about the object. Have each player share his discovery before passing the object to the next player.*

Meet a Tree

A. Direct Experience
B. Empathy, olfactory and tactile awareness
C. Day/forest
D. 2 or more
E. 4 years and up
F. Blindfolds

THIS GAME is for groups of at least two. Pair off. Blindfold your partner and lead him through the forest to any tree that attracts you. (How far will depend on your partner's age and ability to orientate himself. For all but very young children, a distance of 20-30 yards usually isn't too far.)

Help the "blind" child to explore his tree and to feel its uniqueness. I find that specific suggestions are best. For example, if you tell children to *"Feel the tree,"* they won't respond with as much interest as if you say, *"Rub your cheek on the bark."* Instead of, *"Explore your tree,"* be specific: *"Is this tree alive? ... Can you put your arms around it? ... Is the tree older than you are? ... Can you find plants growing on it? ... Animal signs? ... Lichens?"*

When your partner is finished exploring, lead him back to where you began, but take an indirect route. Now, remove the blindfold and let the child try to find the tree with his eyes open. Suddenly, as the child searches for *his* tree, what was a forest becomes a collection of very individual trees.

A tree can be an unforgettable experience in a child's life. Many times children have come back to me a year after we played **Meet a Tree**, and have literally dragged me out to the forest to say, "See! Here's my tree!"

A. Direct Experience
B. Sensory awareness,
   trust
C. Day/anywhere
D. 1 or more
E. 7 years and up
F. Roped trail, blind-
   folds

Blind Trail

ABLIND TRAIL is a rope-guided caravan whose travelers roam through lands full of strange sounds, mysterious smells, and interesting textures. Most travellers can hardly wait to retrace their steps through this enchanted land with eyes open.

To make your blind trail exciting, find an area that offers a variety of experiences. An example of a good **Blind Trail** might be: Follow a shady forest path; climb over a moss-covered log; emerge into a sunlit clearing humming with summer bees; dive again into the forest (this time crawling beneath a dense canopy of six-foot pine saplings), and feel and hear the smooth, dry needles crackle under your hands and knees. The odor of damp vegetation and a chorus of startled ducks announce your arrival at what can only be a pond.

A really good **Blind Trail** takes a fair amount of time to set up; but even a quickly-improvised one can be worthwhile. The important elements to keep in mind are: variety, theme, and mystery. For example, you can create a varied experience of touch, hearing, and smell; or arrange for contrasts within one sense—a rough and a smooth rock; tender new leaves and dry, crackly, dead ones; or a rich, moist odor and a sweet spring fragrance. (Tie a knot in the line to indicate that there's an interesting smell nearby.) Another way to add variety is to make the rope go up and down by attaching it to interesting objects on the ground and overhead.

A specific theme helps to link the various experiences together in the children's minds, especially if you tell them that there will be a special theme. Some possible themes are: tree identification; exploring an animal habitat; or contrasting local climates. (A local climate is a well-defined area—like the sun-shaded north side of a hill—with its own unique conditions of temperature, moisture, and vegetation.) It's easy to include an element of mystery: anything unfamiliar is mysterious. For instance, a string leading away from the main line and descending into a deep hole in a tree is a very good mystery experience.

Before laying out the trail, decide which side of the rope the children will walk on. (Be sure to tell them to stay on that side.) Keep safety in mind and make sure there aren't any poisonous plants or animals in the area.

A calm, receptive mind greatly enhances the child's enjoyment of the trail, so it's very helpful to precede the **Blind Trail** experience with a story or some other quiet activity. Before you start the game, you might guide the children's hands over a tree trunk. Ask them to hug the tree and see how big around it is, and how it feels. Offer them a leaf to smell. Give them some idea of how to explore the trail, so they won't just run through it. Encourage them to be silent as they explore.

Have the children go in intervals to prevent them from bunching up at points along the trail. You can let each child go at his own pace by leading anyone going fast around anyone going especially slow. It's helpful to have a leader or responsible child at the end of the trail, too, in order to greet the children as they finish. (You may want to have other leaders at specific points along the trail as well.)

A fun question to ask the children when they finish (before they've had a chance to look at the trail), is, "How long do you think the trail is?" The children always over-estimate its length because they've experienced life so richly through their heightened senses.

The **Blind Trail** is one of my favorite games. It develops the spirit of receptivity that is needed for every kind of nature experience.

A. Direct Experience
B. Concentration, empathy
C. Day and night/ anywhere
D. 1 or more
E. 4 years and up
F. None

Role Playing

BE A DANDELION parachute, freely drifting. Or a tree; feel your highest branches swaying with the wind's ebb and flow. Become a coyote pup gamboling across a flower-covered clearing; a bear in its winter cave.

Role-playing gets you into the moods, qualities, and behavior of nature's life-forms, grafting them into your self and letting you feel your own heart's and mind's responses to them.

Being a human—John the executive or Sally the shortstop—sometimes gets to be confining. Our enjoyment and appreciation of life depends on our ability to sense the feelings of other creatures, escaping our self-definitions to taste the joy of self-forgetful empathy with others.

Choose an animal, plant, tree, rock or mountain—anything—and pretend you *are* that. Coordinate your body and imagination to experience the existence, movements and feelings of that other form of creation. The warm summer breeze blows across your dragonfly wings as you dance among the water reeds. The snow is soft and cold under your fox-paws; your thick fur is protection against the icy wind, but your empty stomach is growling. You hungrily watch a mouse as it scurries across the snow, stopping every few feet to nose in the frozen grasses.

The more you can put your whole being into pretending, the more you'll take on the character and feelings of your subject. The more deeply you can concentrate, the more oneness and sympathetic understanding you'll feel.

Simple scenes like the dandelion parachute or the swaying tree are best for beginners at role-playing. Group practice is good, too—you'll feel less self-conscious when everyone is doing the same thing around you. Try being a snake or a banana slug inching along; or act out the life-cycle of a beech tree: first the seed in the ground, then gaining strength and stature as you become a mighty adult tree, then the rotting and falling, and finally merging back into the soil from whence you drew your first life. You can act out the whole life cycle in a minute or two. As you gain confidence and concentration you'll have fun with more complicated images:

You are part of a flock of green-winged teal (ducks) that passes just over the marsh grass, then twists and turns upwards. Each teal is attuned to the leader, and the flock moves as if it were one bird. You descend gracefully onto the smooth water.

In a different vein: hold a public hearing on whether to build a dam on a certain river. Lobbyists come to the meeting—a farmer, a fisherman, a trout, a salmon, a deer, a cottonwood tree, a water-strider, a kingfisher, a mosquito, and any others who should be consulted.

Set a supportive and non-critical atmosphere in the role-playing sessions. Let the child develop at his own pace without fear of comparisons or competition.

HOW MUCH CAN YOU SEE?

I n a new environment children au-
tomatically set right out to prove
themselves. They run down steep
hills, and try to climb over, under, and through favored obstacles
like creeks, logs, cliffs and big
rocks. The games in this chapter enlist this kind of adven-
turous spirit to help make children more sensitively aware
of their environment.

Even a simple day-hike can be turned into an adventure, with some learning and increased awareness on the
side. After we've hiked out from camp to our turnaround
point, I'll frequently ask the group if they think they can
find the way back. (On the way out I'll have given them
help by pointing to landmarks and asking them to look
back the way we've come.) There's always a brief period of
shock and confusion when they find out it's up to them to
lead us back. After much consultation and some friendly
argument, a leader and a direction are chosen. Often I'm

accused of turning over the leadership because I don't know
the way back myself. But they nearly always find the way
back without any help from me ... even if it takes all night.

We were out on a night hike once, when we heard a
Great Horned Owl calling from a distance. We decided to
see if we could get close to an owl: but every time we approached, it flew deeper into the forest. Around midnight,
when we still hadn't caught up with the owl, we conceded
that it was time to go back to camp. I asked the boys which
was the best route home, and seven fingers pointed to directions spread around a 230-degree arc of the compass!

There was no chance of rain, and it wasn't very cold
for a high-Sierran night, so I said they could try to find
the way back without my help. The oldest boy took the lead,
and I brought up the rear. But it soon became obvious that
our leader didn't know the way. His status in the group
prevented the others in the group from expressing their
doubts; but when we wound up back where we'd started,
he was quickly deposed and another boy took over the lead.
One after another the leaders were chosen, then hopefully
exchanged, as we wandered around in the forest night.
Finally the boys swallowed their pride and admitted that
they couldn't possibly find their way back in the dark.

I sensed that most of them wanted to sleep out and

keep trying in the morning. Even though we didn't have sleeping bags or warm coats, we decided to get through the night as best we could, huddling together for warmth. We put the ones who were dressed lightest in the middle, and the rest of us piled on and around them.

This worked fine for about thirty minutes, when the ones who were being crushed on the bottom began squirming their way out of the pile. The boys on the outside then seized their chance for a little warmth and wriggled into the middle. Those on top were cold, and those on the bottom were crushed; only while temporarily in the middle of the constantly-shifting downward cycle could any of us stay comfortable and warm.

Four hours of squirming later, a dull gray light in the East promised an end to the struggle. We got up and stomped and danced to stay warm while we waited for the sun.

In daylight it was easy for the group to get their bearings and find the way home. We arrived at camp bleary-eyed, but victorious and proud. A year later the same boys begged me for another overnight bivouac.

You won't necessarily have an experience like this—unless you want to. But the games in this chapter are similar in their ability to make children keenly interested in being as observant of nature as possible.

A. Focus Attention
B. Auditory awareness
C. Day and night/
   anywhere
D. 1 or more
E. 3 years and up
F. None

IN A FOREST, meadow, marsh or park, a group of children sit or lie down on their backs with both fists held up in the air. Every time someone hears a new bird song he lifts one finger. Who has the best hearing? This is a wonderful way to make children aware of the sounds (and the stillness) of nature. For fun, see if you can count to ten without hearing a bird song. Vary the game by listening for general animal

sounds—or for any sounds at all, like wind in the grass, falling leaves, rushing water. See if you can follow the wind as it flows through the forest.

To get children to concentrate more deeply on any natural setting, ask them how many different colors and shades of colors they can see in front of them without moving from where they are standing.

Sounds & Colors

THIS GAME is played to introduce the concepts of protective coloration and adaptation, as well as to enhance children's observational skills. A benefit of this increased visual awareness is that children become much more careful about littering outdoors.

Look for a trail going through an area where you can see the ground and where there isn't a lot of tall grass or thick shrubs. (A forest where there are both small and large trees, leaf litter, rotting logs, and some plants is ideal.) Choose a 65 to 100-foot section of the trail making sure that it is wide enough for two people to pass. Along the trail you'll place 16 to 24 man-made objects. Some of them should stand out, like brightly-colored balloons or fluorescent pink cockroaches. Others should blend with their surroundings, and therefore be more difficult to pick out. Keep the number of objects you've planted secret.

The children walk over the section of trail one at a time, with intervals between them, trying to spot (but not pick up) as many of the objects as they can. When they reach the end of the trail, they whisper in your ear how many they saw. Tell each child the total number of objects, or, if you prefer, the fraction or percent of the total that

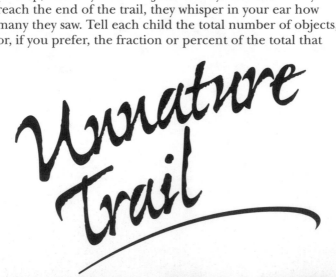

Unnature Trail

A. Focus Attention
B. Camouflage, visual
   awareness
C. Day/forest, thicket
D. 1-30
E. 5-13 years
F. Man-made litter

they've found. Encourage the children to walk the trail again, looking for any objects they've missed. If you want to make it easier for the players, place a marker (like a red bandanna) near the objects that are the hardest to find.

In setting up, I've found it's helpful to use rope to mark the side of the trail where the objects are hidden. Then place the objects no further than four feet beyond the rope (make sure to tell the players this). You can, however, hide the objects at different heights, and in places where they can be seen only if you turn and look backwards. This helps the children break out of the habit of looking only straight ahead. If you have a large group, be sure to make the trail long enough so that everyone can be on the trail at once. It's also helpful to ask half the group to begin along the middle of the trail, and then come back and finish the first half. This way no one has to wait in line too long.

To challenge older children, and keep them interested, it's important to have some objects that are placed in plain view, but are still difficult to find. One of my favorites is a 3 x 4 inch camping mirror. When its top edge is tilted toward you, the mirror reflects only the forest litter, making it blend in perfectly with its surroundings. (Lay a small branch over the top of the mirror to cover its edge and to hold it upright.) Often I've had as many as fifteen people kneeling and standing right in front of the mirror, gazing intently, but not seeing it, until I've touched the mirror. Objects like rusty chains, nails, rubber bands, and clothes pegs work well, too.

To allow everyone to see where the objects were hidden, go to the beginning of the trail, and start walking along the rope, and have the players (who are standing further back) point out the objects as you go by each one. As you pick up the objects, have a designated player collect them, and another player count out the number of objects found as you go along.

End the game with a discussion of the ways camouflage coloration helps animals. Then go on a search for small camouflaged animals (insects, spiders, etc.).

A. Focus Attention
B. Concentration, exploring sensory awareness
C. Day/forest, thicket
D. 2-5 (per leader)
E. 6 years and up
F. Blindfolds

TAKE YOUR children to a secluded, secret spot. After blindfolding them, arrange them in a line, caterpillar-fashion, with each child placing his hands on the shoulders of the child ahead of him. Tell them that as you lead them along they are to listen to, smell, and feel their surroundings as completely as they can. Make frequent stops along the way at points of interest, such as unusual trees and rocks, or to smell a fragrant flower or bush. The more variety there is along the route, the better. To add variety, walk on and off trails, follow a dry stream bed, or go in and out of sunny forest clearings.

When you have gone as far as you think is appropriate, remove the blindfolds. The children must now try to find their way back along the route to the starting point. Sometimes, before they start back I'll ask them to draw a picture or map of what they think the course and the areas we passed through look like. This helps them to translate into pictures the sounds, smells, and touches they've experienced. The sound of ducks might indicate a pond or marsh; fragrance would mean flowers. As much as possible, allow the children to find the way back on their own.

Caution: blind caterpillars more than five segments long become quickly entangled and hard to manage.

Caterpillar Walk

A. Direct Experience
B. Exploring, orienting, sensory awareness
C. Day/anywhere
D. 2 or more
E. 6 years and up
F. Blindfolds

THIS IS a shorter version of **Caterpillar Walk**. Blindfold your children and tell them you are going to lead them to a spot not too far away. Ask them to explore their surroundings with their hands until they know the spot well. When they are satisfied, lead them back—still blindfolded—to the starting point. Take the blindfold off and ask them to find the spot they explored with their hands.

& Back Home

THIS IS A GOOD GAME for getting children interested in rocks, plants, and animals. Before assembling the children to play, secretly gather from the immediate area about 10 common natural objects, such as rocks, seeds, conifer cones, plant parts, and some signs of animal activity. Lay the objects out on a handkerchief and cover them with another handkerchief. Call the children close around you and tell them, *"Under this cloth are 10 natural objects that you'll be able to find nearby. I will lift the handkerchief for 25 seconds so you can take a good look and try to remember everything you see."*

After looking at the objects, the children spread out and collect identical items, keeping their findings to themselves. After five minutes of searching, call them back. Dramatically pull the objects from under the handkerchief, one at a time, telling interesting stories about each one. As each object is presented, ask the children if they found one just like it.

Children have a lively curiosity about the kinds of things you'll show them—rocks, seeds, plants, and so on. When you repeat the game several times, it has a notice-able strengthening effect on the child's concentration and memory.

Duplication

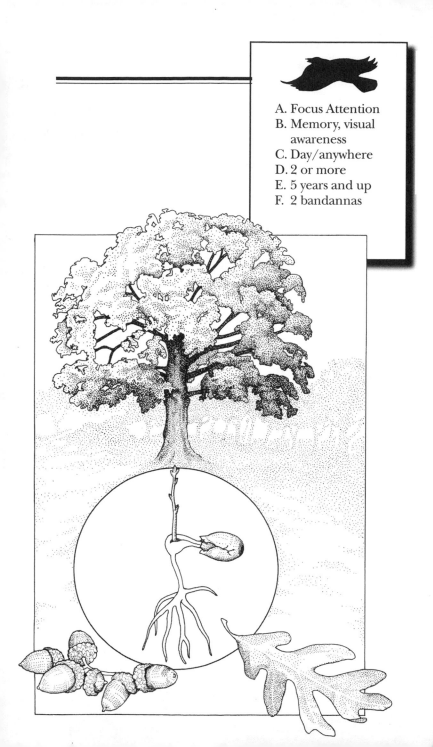

A. Focus Attention
B. Memory, visual awareness
C. Day/anywhere
D. 2 or more
E. 5 years and up
F. 2 bandannas

A. Focus Attention
B. Observation of soil surface
C. Day/anywhere
D. 1 or more
E. 4 years and up
F. 3'-5' strings, magnifying glasses

Micro-Hike

A **MICRO-HIKE** is a very short expedition guided by a string three to five feet long. The "hikers" cover the trail inch by inch on their bellies, viewing such natural wonders as grass blades bent by rainbow dewdrops, colorful beetles sprinkled with flower pollen, and powerful-jawed eight-eyed spiders. Because young children are particularly fond of tiny objects, their interest absorption in the world of the forest-in-miniature will amaze you.

Begin by asking the children to span their strings over

the most interesting ground they can find. Give each child a magical magnifying glass, to shrink himself down to the size of an ant. You may want to ask them questions to stimulate their imaginations: *"What kind of world are you traveling through right now? Who are your nearest neighbors? Are they friendly? Do they work hard? What is that spider going to do—eat you, or take you for a ride? What would it be like to be that metallic green beetle? How does he spend his day?"*

At the start, tell the children that they must keep their eyes no higher than one foot above the ground.

NATURE'S BALANCE

owadays, children get lots of instruction in textbook concepts of ecology. By contrast, the main emphasis in this book is on developing their heart and intuitive qualities. Yet feelings alone sometimes aren't enough, especially when those feelings aren't shared by others. Years ago I had an experience that first made me aware of this truth. It also caused me to want to balance my intuitive understanding of nature with a stronger scientific background.

At the back of the farm where I lived was a small brush-covered slough (a piece of low, muddy, swampy land). I spent most of my free hours there, and another creature came there often, too—a Red Tail Hawk. I'd find her roosting on one of the dead oaks, where she liked to perch for the unobstructed view of the surrounding area. After several months she became so used to me that she'd stay on her perch even when I walked close by her.

During the day I was in the habit of climbing to the farmhouse roof to look out over the almond orchards at the surrounding country. From there I could also see if the

Red Tail was at her post, 150 yards away. As the months passed, a feeling of friendship developed between us.

One morning just after I'd returned from a few days' absence, I walked out to the slough to see if everything was okay. To my shock, I found that all of the oaks were downed and burning, and that a man was just getting set to fell the last tree—the hawk's favorite.

I tried to persuade him to leave the tree standing, but he said it wasn't doing any good so he might as well cut it down and burn it. I said there wasn't any possibility of its falling on an almond tree, and because it was dead it wasn't using up any water or soil nutrients. But he wouldn't be moved, and the tree was on his land, so there wasn't much else I could do. After the oaks were cut down I rarely saw the Red Tail hawk again.

My heart had spoken to the tree-cutter, but I didn't have the facts to support my feelings. I felt there must be some important reasons why dead trees are valuable; but at the time I didn't know any of those reasons. Later, I did find information that might have helped him understand the possible negative consequences of chopping down those oaks. For instance, dead trees provide homes for many birds—like woodpeckers and nuthatches—that rid the land of harmful insect pests.

THIS GAME requires at least six players. Give each child a slip of paper and have him secretly write on it the name of a plant or animal that lives in the area. The players are going to build a pyramid, just as they might do in gym glass; but don't tell them this until after you've collected all the slips of paper. Now the fun begins: *"From what source does*

Pyramid of Life

A. Awaken Enthusiasm
B. Balance of nature, food chain
C. Day/clearing
D. 6 or more
E. 7 years and up
F. Pencils & paper, plant & animal names on cards

the Earth get its energy? ... From the sun! ... Right. What form of life is the first to make use of that energy? ... Plants! ... Right again. Now we're going to build a pyramid."

A few groans may be heard when the "plant children" realize their fate.

"The plants will be on the bottom, because all animals depend on them directly or indirectly for food. All the plants kneel down here on all fours, close together in a line. Now, as I read off the animals from the slips of paper, tell me whether they are plant-eaters or meat-eaters. All the plant-eaters (herbivores) stand in a line behind the plants. All the meat-eaters (carnivores) stand in another line behind the herbivores.

There will nearly always be more children in the upper-level groups than in the supporting plant levels; it's a lot more fun to be a bear or mountain lion than it is to be a dandelion or a muskrat. Humility, alas, seldom stimulates the imagination. With so many tops and so few bottoms, it will be impossible to build a stable pyramid. Some of the predators will just have to forfeit their exalted status. Challenge the children to reconstruct their own pyramid into one that will easily support all its members. (Tell them the bigger children can change to plants if they wish.) Clearly, the higher up in the food chain, the fewer the number of animals there are. Demonstrate the importance of plants by pretending to pull one of them out of the pyramid.

Another way to play the **Pyramid Game** is to hand out to each player a card with the name of a plant or animal written on it. It's more fun if you choose interesting and amusing plant and animal names—like baby blue eyes, Virginia spring beauty, common horsetail, and hog-nosed snake. If possible, have all the animals and plants be from the same habitat. Writing down the names on the cards also allows you to fix the ratio of plants, herbivores, and predators. Along with the name of a plant or animal, write on each card a Roman numeral (plants, I; herbivores, II; predators, III; and a large predator, IV). For a group of twenty-six players a suggested ratio (plants to top predator) is, 14 - 7 - 4 - 1.

Shuffle the cards and pass one card to each player. If any players aren't sure what row to go to, they can look to see what Roman numeral they have. Here's how to play: "*I'd like everyone who can make food from the sun, air, water and trace minerals to come forward and kneel in a long line.....
Would all the plants please introduce themselves?.....* (The plant players respond with their fun plant names like, black-eyed Susan!,....Northern lady fern!,.... touch-me-not!, amidst great laughter.) *Now, herbivores, come and stand behind the plants. Tell us who you are..... If you're a predator, make a third row and identify yourselves..... Is there anyone who lives at the very top of the food chain? Yes? Please tell us who you are? ... A bald eagle, ... then come and be the fourth row.* Now that you have everyone in place, pretend that you are going to build a pyramid. (I say only pretend because its a little risky to build one with this many people.)

Explain to the group that there is a model in science

that says that every time you go from one level to a higher one (i.e., plants to herbivores), only 1/10 of the biomass is retained. So for example, if you have one thousand pounds of plants, you'd have one hundred pounds of herbivores, ten of predators, and one of the top predator.

Now tell the group: *"I've noticed that the plants are having trouble with some insects, so I'm going to spray with a pesticide. These bandannas that I'm placing on your heads— one per plant—signify a particle of poison..... Now I'd like the herbivores to reach down and eat the plants. You do this by taking the plant's bandanna and putting it on the top of your head. Keep eating until all the plants are eaten.*

"Poisons like herbicides and pesticides are dangerous to animals because when they're digested the poison stays in the animal's tissue. Let's now have the predators eat the herbivores..... " (By now the players see where the game is going and are greatly anticipating what will happen when all the bandannas reach the fourth row.) *"Now would the bald eagle eat the animals in the third row?"* (The players laugh as the bald eagle-player now wears a large pile of bandannas as a hat.) *"As we go higher up the food chain, more and more poison concentrates in the tissues of the animals. This process is called biological magnification. Birds like eagles, peregrine falcons, and pelicans and other animals, too, have been greatly harmed by poisons in the environment.....Where do you, as a human, fit into the food chain?"*

GIVE EACH CHILD an imaginary deed to one square mile of land. On this virgin plot he will be free to create his own dream-forest, complete with as many trees, animals, mountains and rivers as he desires. Let their imaginations run wild. To encourage creativity you can give the children some suggestions:

"To make your forest beautiful and radiant, you might want to add things like waterfalls and windstorms,

Recipe for

A. Share Inspiration
B. Aesthetic apprecia-
   tion, balance of
   nature
C. Day/forest
D. 2 or more
E. 7 years and up
F. Pencils and index
   cards

or perpetual rainbows...."

Have them list the ingredients of their forest, then have them draw a picture of it. End by discussing with them whether their individual forests are able to maintain themselves year after year. For instance, see if they have chosen representatives of the food cycle: plant-eaters, plants, and decomposers (example: ants, mushrooms, bacteria). Don't let them forget subtle factors like soil and climate.

a Forest

A. Awaken Enthusiasm
B. Adaptation, habitat,
   interdependence
C. Day/anywhere
D. 3 or more
E. 5 years and up
F. Ball of string

Webbing

HERE IS A GAME that makes very clear the
essential interrelationships among all the
members of nature's community. Webbing
vividly portrays how air, rocks, plants, and
animals function together in a balanced web of life.

The children form a circle. The leader stands inside
the circle near the edge, with a ball of string: *"Who can
name a plant that grows in this area? ... Brodiaea ... Good. Here,
Miss Brodiaea, you hold the end of the string. Is there an animal
living around here that might eat the brodiaea? ... Rabbits? ... Ah,
a sumptuous meal. Mr. Rabbit, you take hold of the string here;
you are connected to Miss Brodiaea by your dependence on her
flowers for your lunch. Now, who needs Mr. Rabbit for his lunch?"*

Continue connecting the children with string as their

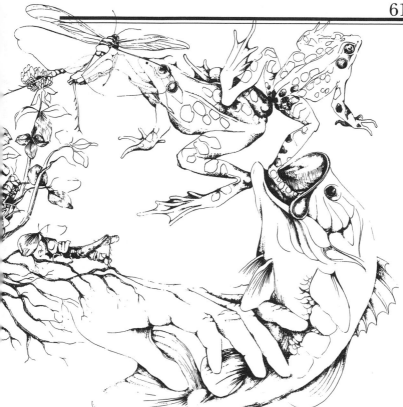

relationships to the rest of the group emerge. Bring in new elements and considerations, such as other animals, soil, water and so on, until the entire circle of children is strung together in a symbol of the web of life. You have created your own ecosystem.

To demonstrate how each individual is important to the whole community, take away by some plausible means one member of the web. For example, a fire or a logger kills a tree. When the tree falls, it tugs on the strings it holds; anyone who feels a tug in his string is in some way affected by the death of the tree. Now everyone who felt a tug from the tree gives a tug. The process continues until every individual is shown to be affected by the destruction of the tree.

Predator-

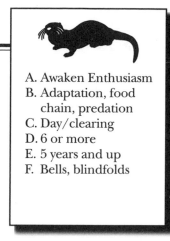

A. Awaken Enthusiasm
B. Adaptation, food chain, predation
C. Day/clearing
D. 6 or more
E. 5 years and up
F. Bells, blindfolds

This game introduces food chains and the way they work in nature. In an open clearing, form a circle about 15 feet across. Blindfold two of the children and have them stand in the center of the circle. Ask one of the children to name a predator that lives in the area, and ask the other child to name a prey. The predator tries to catch his prey by listening for him, then tracking him down and tagging him. If either animal goes too near the edge of the circle, the children tap him twice. Stress the need for silence while the game is in progress, and have the players make things more realistic by imitating the animals they've chosen to be. For variety, experiment with different numbers of predators and prey. Put bells on some of the animals, forcing them to modify their strategy of hunting or of avoiding capture. If your predator is not as bold as he could be, and interest is lagging, tighten up the circle, bringing the predator and his prey closer together.

Prey

A. Focus Attention
B. Adaptation, habitat, plant succession
C. Day/pond edge
D. 1 or more
E. 10 years and up
F. Pencils and paper

Plant Succession Crawl

PLANT succession is the process by which soil and water conditions of an area gradually change, allowing new species to come in and eventually establish themselves, and forcing old species to migrate to more favorable conditions. A very good place for observing plant succession is the area close around a pond, especially if there is a gentle slope running up away from the water. As you move farther away from the center, the soil becomes drier and its composition changes. You will be able to observe several plant types in successive rings around the pond.

To see the actual process of plant succession, you would have to watch the changes in and around a pond over a period of many years. This is because plant succession is the result of plants dying and slowly building up and drying out the soil. When the soil becomes drier, the plants that like wet soil are easily forced out by their dry-soil competitors. Over a long period a pond will actually shrink and disappear as the soil level builds up higher

and   higher
around it. The rings
of plant life move gradually
closer to the center of the pond
as the wet area becomes smaller.
You can see this process of plant mi-
gration happening by careful observation at any one of its points; it is rather like
looking at one frame of a movie film.

Have the children crawl from the outside
rings toward the edge of the water. By crawling
and closely examining the ground, they will get a
feeling for the different soil conditions needed
by the different types of plants in the rings. Ask
the children to share their discoveries as they find
them. One discovery might be coming across a
new ring with its special kinds of trees, shrubs,
plants and grasses, or wetter and stronger-smell-
ing soil. When he reaches the water, have each
child draw a map of the pond and its surrounding area, with the successive circles
of plant life. Label each ring from
wettest to driest, and list the plants
that grow there. Ask the children
to imagine how big the pond
will be in fifty or a
hundred years.

LEARNING IS FUN

I *try my best to make learning fun and exciting for children. One way I do this is to point out characteristics that animals and plants have in common with man. Before taking children to a pond, for instance, I'll talk with them for awhile about aquatic insects.*

"What things do humans use to help them move and breathe in water?"

"Fins. Wet suits. Air tanks. Oars. Nets. Diving masks."

"Did you know that aquatic insects have the same needs, and use the same equipment, as man does? For example, there are diving beetles that use scuba tanks: they trap a silvery bubble of air under a thick layer of hair, then use it to breathe underwater. Some diving beetles even carry an air-bubble 'tank' along behind them. A beetle's breathing system is more efficient than our scuba tanks, though, because beetles don't need compressed air, and they can fill their tanks with oxygen

from the surrounding water. With his diving tank, a beetle can stay underwater for as long as thirty-six hours! Diving beetles also have waxy hairs that make them float—just like a wet suit. If they aren't swimming or holding onto something, they bob right up to the surface.

"Most aquatic insects use the breast stroke when they swim, although a few prefer the crawl. But there is one insect who likes the backstroke so much that he's been named the 'back swimmer.' He is shaped like a boat, with a keel running down his back and two long, oar-like legs at his sides.

"Then there is the black fly larva, who lives in the fast riffles of a stream. He moves along carefully while fastened to a safety rope. If the stream carries him away, he can crawl back along the rope to his original position. The black fly larva often reaches adult size while still underwater. To keep his wings from getting wet he rides up out of the water inside a bubble of air—like a submarine!"

Children are captivated by bizarre tales of these underwater creatures. They're always excited by the chance to comb through aquatic vegetation for bugs with kitchen strainers. Once the search begins, I find myself bounding from one shriek of delight to another as they call to me to come and see their findings.

A class of sixth-graders had just finished hunting for insects, when a water truck drove up to the tiny pond and lowered its hose into the water. When the driver started his pump, the children immediately realized that the insects would later be spread out on the road, and die. So several of them went up to the driver and pleaded with him to put a fine screen over the hose. The man was friendly; touched by the children's concern, he said he would be happy to install the screen. Afterwards the children introduced him to their aquatic friends.

It's fascinating to discover how different life forms live. The games in this chapter create an atmosphere of excitement that stimulates the child's curiosity and concentration.

A. Awaken Enthusiasm
B. Natural history
C. Day or night/
   anywhere
D. 2 or more
E. 5 years and up
F. None

THE **NOSES** GAME creates a wonderful sense of fun and mystery. In this game of discovery, the answer to a riddle gradually comes into focus for the players. Playing **Noses** is a great way to capture the attention and enthusiasm of a group right from the start of your class and to engage them fully in the learning process. Here is how to play:

"I am going to read eight clues for an animal and you are to try to guess its identity. Of course, if you say the answer out loud, it will give the answer away. So when you think you know the animal, I'd like you to give me a signal. The signal is putting your finger on your nose. This will tell me—and also everybody else—that you know the answer.

"Let's say for example, in the first clue that you have spots. Aha, you think, I'm a baby deer! So you put your finger on your nose..... But you find out in the second clue that you are swimming upstream to lay your eggs. You're in trouble, aren't you? Well, you can make a cough and cover your mouth or start scratching your head, and pretend your finger wasn't anywhere near your nose. This way no one will know that you were wrong!

"You can help each other and whisper to those closest to you, just don't let your voices carry across the room. The animal is one you know, but may not be one that lives in this region. Don't worry if you don't know the answer right away, because the clues get easier and easier as we go. Forget about the first two clues (the spots and swimming upstream); they were just examples.

"Clue number one is: 'I live everywhere except polar regions, oceans, and very dry deserts.' (Pause) Number two is: 'I have been known to live for 32 years. That's helpful because I have a slow reproductive rate. I have one young every year.' (Pause) Three is: 'In the United States, four out of every ten species are threatened or endangered.' (Pause) Four is: 'Most of us have excellent hearing, but some of us rely more on sight and smell.' (Pause) I see some fingers on

some noses, that's good. *Clue five is more helpful and informative: 'My wingspan varies from seven inches to six feet. I have been known to fly up to two miles high. One of my kind can eat up to 600 mosquitoes an hour.' Ah, I see we lost several noses; but we gained some new ones, too. The rest of you must be waiting to guess the subspecies! Six is: 'I have small or big ears, often a tiny tail, live alone or in groups. Many of us eat insects, while others eat pollen, or fruit, or even fish and frogs!' (Pause) I see more noses....there's one over here... and there....well, the next clue is going to help a lot: 'We're called masters of the night sky. There are more kinds of us than of any other mammal. If cold weather comes, we may migrate or hibernate.' More noses! That's great. Clue eight is: 'Most of us (in the United States) find our way by making high pitched sounds and listening for their return. I rest, head down, feet up.' It looks like everybody knows the answer. Say it out loud on three, one.... two.... three....(the players shout .... Bat!)"*

Please see pages 159 to 163 for more riddles for the **Noses** game.

Noses

A. Awaken Enthusiasm
B. Animal classification, animal ecology
C. Day/clearing or road
D. 4 - 16
E. 7 years and up
F. Rope, pencils, paper, 2 bandannas

THE **ANIMAL GAME** is an entertaining way to review zoology and animal ecology. Dramatic climaxes surprise the players again and again, and make for lots of excitement and laughter. It's a great rainy day activity and excellent for encouraging reading and looking through field guides.

Form two equal teams of up to eight players each. Give each team a piece of paper and pencil. Each team chooses an animal and then thinks up, and writes down, six to eight riddle clues for that animal.

(Encourage teams to select an animal

Animal Game

the other team knows, but won't think of immediately.) The clues should be progressively easier, proceeding from the general to the specific, with the last clue making the animal's identity obvious. You'll find a list of sample clues below.

When both teams have their clues ready, have them face each other across a line made by a rope. Fifteen feet behind each team place a bandanna, which will be that team's home base. Tell the players they have to just run past home base—not stand on it. (See diagram on the next page.)

One team gives their clues for their animal first, and the other team tries to guess. The guessing team is allowed only one guess per clue. Once the animal is guessed, the other team gives their clues.

Here is how the game is played: Team A gives its first clue; then team B tries to guess the identity of Team A's animal. If the guess is wrong, the clue reader from Team A answers "No!" and nothing happens. Now the second person in line on team A gives his team's second clue, and team B guesses again, but it's incorrect, too, so still nothing happens. As the clues become more and more obvious, the tension mounts. This continues until someone on team B guesses correctly. For example, the clue reader on team A says, "I have three toes," and team B guesses, "Are you a black-backed, three-toed woodpecker?"

The members of team A turn nervously toward home base, while team B hovers eagerly over them. But team A can't run home until their clue reader says "Yes." Then "Yes" is shouted and team A streaks for home base with team B in hot pursuit.

It's important to remind the players that only the clue reader is to answer. The rest of the team shouldn't start running until the clue reader responds "Yes" to a correct guess. Also the clue reader should reply to only the first guess, even if a following one is correct. Any player on the guessing team can shout out a guess.

The first time children play, it's difficult to restrain them from running for home base once the other team guesses their animal and *before* "Yes" is called out. I have fun "penalizing" the offending early runners by bringing them back and making them put one foot over the rope and playing the game again. This way the opposite team gets a fair chance of chasing them, and the players learn the habit of waiting until "Yes" is called out. The players learn quickly (usually after one or two times) not to run early.

A simpler and quicker way to play this game is to have all the children line up on one side of the rope with the teachers (who'll be giving the clues) on the other side. There is great anticipation on the children's part as they line up eagerly to chase the teachers.

Here are some sample clues that will give you an idea of the thought processes a child goes through in playing this game. Take a piece of paper and cover all the clues except the first. After you read the clue, try to guess the answer. Continue down the page until you've gone through all the clues. Check your final guess against the coded answer. To decipher the code, write down the letters that follow alphabetically the letters in the code. You'll find nine more sets of clues in the Appendix.

Example: C N F = D O G

1. I have four feet, and my body temperature stays the same.
2. I use my tail as a rudder.
3. My habitat is the forest.
4. My front teeth are constantly growing, so I gnaw a lot.
5. I store no food for the winter like my cousins do. My diet includes nuts, seeds, tree buds, insects, fungi, and some animal flesh.
6. Owls are one of the few animals that can catch me.
7. I go through the air, but I don't fly.
8. I have skin flaps that extend along each side of my body between my ankles and wrists.

E K X H M F   R P T H Q Q D K

Team A's Home Base
X
A A A A A A A
_____
B B B B B B B
X
Team B's Home Base

A. Awaken Enthusiasm
B. Animal classification, animal ecology
C. Day/anywhere
D. 2 or more
E. 6 years and up
F. Animal pictures, clothes pins

What Animal Am I?

PIN A PICTURE of an animal on the back of one of the children in the group. Don't show him the picture. Have him turn around so that all the other children can see what animal he has become. He then asks questions to discover his own identity. The other children can answer only yes, no, and maybe.

A. Awaken Enthusiasm
B. Tree identification
C. Day/clearing or
   road
D. 6 or more
E. 7 years and up
F. Tree specimens

THIS GAME is a lot like Steal the Bacon, but it has been adapted to help children identify and remember the trees and shrubs in an area. As you explore the locale where you'll be playing the game, collect small samples of leaves, flowers, and seeds from the trees and bushes—you'll need about 7 to 10 specimens in all.

Form two equal teams and line them up facing each other, 30 feet apart. Put the plant specimens in a row on the ground between the two teams. The teams count off separately, so that each player has a number, and on each team there are players numbered one, two, three, etc.

When the teams are ready, call out the name of a tree or bush represented by one of the specimens lying between the teams, then call out a number. (To add surprise, call the numbers out of sequence.)

"The next plant is a beech tree, and the number is ... three!"

As soon as the "threes" hear their number called, they race to the specimens, trying to be first to find the beech twig. Every successful player earns two points for his team. Picking up the wrong specimen results in a loss of two points.

Identification Game

A. Awaken Enthusiasm
B. Review of concepts
C. Day/clearing or
   road
D. 6 or more
E. 5-13 years
F. Rope, 2 blindfolds
   (of different color)

THIS IS AN excellent game for reviewing newly-learned concepts. Divide the group into two equal teams, the Owls and the Crows. Have the teams line up facing each other about four feet apart. Place a rope between them. About 15 feet behind each team, place a bandanna which designates Home Base. The leader makes a statement aloud, and if the statement is true the Owls chase the Crows, trying to catch them before they reach their Home Base. If the statement is false, the Crows chase the Owls. Anyone caught must join the other team. Before you begin, practice by giving a few easy statements, and asking the players to just point to where they'll run.

Since the players will be continually changing sides, it's helpful to mark clearly the way to run if the statement's true or false. You can use a blue bandanna to signify the true direction—"true blue" and a red one to show false. Or you can use signs or natural features and say something like "true tree" or "false fence."

If the answer isn't obvious to the players, or they forget which way to run, you'll get some of the Owls and Crows running toward each other, and others running back to their Home Bases. During the pandemonium, the leader should remain silent and neutral. When the action has calmed down, he can reveal the correct answer.

Your statements, however, should be as precise and accurate as possible for the age and experience of the players. For example, if you say *the sun rises in the east*, would that be true? For younger children it might be. But older students probably know that it is the Earth's rotation that makes it appear that the sun is rising.

Here are some sample statements: Sensory: *"The wind is coming from behind the Crows."* Conceptual: *"A deciduous tree keeps*

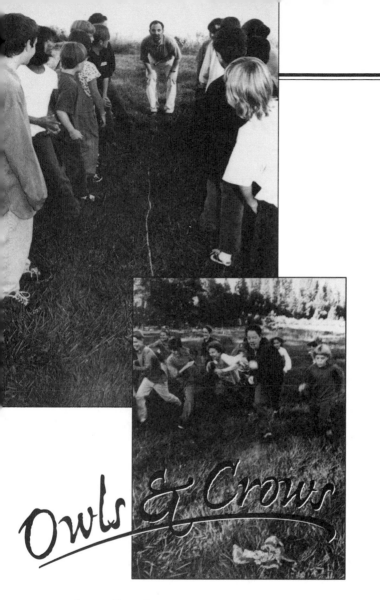

Owls & Crows

its leaves all year long." Observational: (after showing them a leaf) *"The leaf had five points and five veins."* Identification: *"This seed comes from an oak tree."* Other statements you might want to use are: *warm air rises; habitat ... means where a plant or animal lives; birds have teeth;* and, *ducks, turtles and squirrels are warm-blooded.*

Find Your Age

I N THIS ACTIVITY each person tries to find a tree his own age. It's easy to estimate how many years a young pine, spruce, larch or fir tree has, by counting its whorls of branches. In these trees you can see where one year's growth of branches all radiate out from the same band. Simply count the sets of branches and you'll have the approximate age of the tree. Be sure to add extra years for the branch whorls the trees has probably lost at its base. If you look closely you may be able to see scars where the old branches have broken off.

You'll find the best-shaped young trees growing in open clearings, well away from the larger, more dominant trees. (This activity only works with trees up to about 25 years old, because as they grow older, it's difficult to estimate their age.)

Tell the players how a conifer tree grows—from the tip upwards. Each year's new growth grows beyond last year's tip which stays at the same height. The youngest part of the tree is at the very top, while the oldest is at the bottom. The tree also grows from the tips of its branches and roots, as well as a little in diameter at the trunk each year. The trunk doesn't grow any higher, but stays at the same height. To see if the players understand this, you can ask the following question: *"If I nailed a board five feet high on a tree, how much higher would it be after 30 years?"* If they think the board will be higher, asked them if they've ever seen a barbwire fence nailed to a tree—hanging twenty-feet above the ground!

To begin, write down the age of everyone in the group on a piece of paper. Then as a group look for trees that are the approximate age for each of the players. After this is done, have each player spend time studying his tree to see if he can tell anything about its growth and life. For example, I was studying a twenty-year old ponderosa pine, when I discovered I could

A. Direct Experience
B. Tree identification and biology, empathy
C. Day/forest
D. 1 or more
E. 5 years and up
F. Paper and pencil

see the history of northern California's rainfall reflected in its growth. Counting back in years from the top of the tree, I could see energetic growth between the branch whorls during rainy years, and little growth during the drought of the 80's.

Other things you can look for are fire scars; places where animals have used the tree, like deer rubbing their antlers, or bird nests; where another branch has taken over for a tip that was damaged (look for a bend in the trunk); and how its surroundings may have affected the tree.

After giving players time to get to know their tree, have each of them write a letter to their woodland friend. Then have everyone share what they've learned and felt about their special tree. In addition to teaching science, this activity encourages a wonderful sense of empathy and appreciation for trees and their lives.

Tree Silhouettes

"This is the noblest pine...., surpassing all others not merely in size but also in kingly beauty and majesty. It towers sublimely from every ridge and canyon of the range.... No other pine seems to me so unfamiliar and self-contained. In approaching it, we feel as if in the presence of a superior being, and begin to walk with a light step, holding our breath."
—John Muir, describing sugar pines

A FOREST is comprised of many different kinds of trees, making wonderful patterns of distinct shapes and sizes. Playing **Tree Silhouettes** helps children see the trees from the forest, and discover how unique each species is.

A. Awaken Enthusiasm
B. Adaptation, tree profiles
C. Day/forest
D. 2 or more
E. 5 years and up
F. None

Find a place where a variety of trees are growing. Pick a nearby tree that has a distinct silhouette (like a weeping willow or fir). A favorite tree I like to portray is the sugar pine. These tall, stately pines have trunks clear of branches for much of their height. About two thirds up, large lower branches grow straight out from the trunk. And at the tips of these branches, hang cones, 13 to 20 inches long.

Now shape your body to look like the type of tree you've selected. It's okay to make several movements to demonstrate, for example, the tree's lower branches, its trunk, and its leaves. Ask the children if they can guess what kind of tree you are. (You may need to help them with their guesses!) Then ask if they can point out a tree of the type you've acted out.

Now that the children know how to play, divide them up into two groups, and have each group go off to observe the trees in the area. From their study, each group chooses the trees they want to portray to the other group. A whole team can portray a tree, or the group can choose a member who most resembles the species they want to represent.

Bring the two teams together and have each team alternate portraying their trees. After the groups have finished, it's an opportune time to share inspiring passages about trees. John Muir, Donald Culross Peattie, and many others have written beautifully about different kinds of trees. The children will be interested in knowing more about the trees they observed and acted out, or saw portrayed.

A. Focus Attention
B. Ecology, identifica-
   tion, observation
C. Day/anywhere
D. 3 or more
E. 5-14 years
F. Paper sacks, pencils,
   scavenger lists

Scavenger Hunt

SCAVENGER HUNTS are probably familiar to you from your own childhood. This one is adapted to finding natural objects. You should assign scavenger lists that require the child to think creatively or to look very closely. Given here is a scavenger list adapted from the one used at the Glen Helen Outdoor Education Center in Yellow Springs, Ohio.

*17. Everything in nature has a function. *21. Everything in nature is important (even poison oak is important to the birds that eat its berries). *24. A sun trap is anything that captures the sun's heat (water, rocks, plants, animals).

Scavenger List

Collect only things that you can return safely and without damage.

1. A feather
2. One seed dispersed by the wind
3. Exactly 100 of something
4. A maple leaf
5. A thorn
6. A bone
7. Three different kinds of seeds
8. One camouflaged animal or insect
9. Something round
10. Part of an egg
11. Something fuzzy
12. Something sharp
13. A piece of fur
14. Five pieces of man-made litter
15. Something perfectly straight
16. Something beautiful
17. Something that is of no use in nature*
18. A chewed leaf, (not by you!)
19. Something that makes a noise
20. Something white
21. Something important in nature*
22. Something that reminds you of yourself
23. Something soft
24. A sun trap*
25. A big smile

Wild Animal Scramble

CHILDREN show keen interest in animals and their lives when you introduce them through the **Wild Animal Scramble**.

Write the names of common animals on index cards. (Pictures are even better, if available, because they stimulate more interest and enable the players to give more accurate responses.) Pin one animal picture or name on the back of each player's collar. At your signal, the players begin asking questions to get clues to their own identities. Encourage them to ask only one question of each person and have that person ask one question of them, so they interact with everyone in the group. Answers are limited to yes, no, maybe, and "I don't know." (This last answer is an important one. Players can be thrown off the track by incorrect answers to their questions.)

Remind the players to ask questions to discover characteristics about their animal. For example, asking questions like, *"Do I have wings?"* makes the game more educational, than, *"Am I a butterfly?"* (For first time players, it's also helpful to give examples of different types of questions that will help them discover their animal.)

To give everyone a feeling of success, let each player's knowledge be the criteria for how specific his answer should be. For example, for a very young child, *bird* would be a good answer. For someone knowing many different

A. Awaken Enthusiasm
B. Animal classifica-
   tion, animal ecology
C. Day and night/
   anywhere
D. 4 or more
E. 7 years and up
F. Animal pictures,
   clothes pins

kinds of birds, *sparrow* could be correct. An avid bird watcher might want to be more specific, so, *song sparrow*, or even one of its subspecies, would be the right answer.

As soon as each player feels certain that he knows the name of his animal, he can guess, *"Am I a ......?"* If he's right, have him pin the picture to the front of his shirt; this way you'll know who's finished and who isn't.

Besides teaching the concept of animal classification, this game also helps bring out three important qualities:

1. Open-mindedness: avoiding preconceptions and snap judgments. *"Let's see, I live in the forest; I'm warm-blooded; I'm active at night, and I can fly. Well, that means I'm a bird."* (Actually, the correct answer might have been *a flying squirrel* or *bat*.)

2. Discrimination: using new information, and testing the validity of new information. Some examples: *(a) "I can swim, and I'm warm-blooded. (Then I have to be a bird or a mammal. What birds and mammals swim?)" (b) "Jerry told me I'm a member of the rodent family? But I'm a predator. I think I can discount Jerry's answer, because no rodents are predators. Besides, I have dog-like tracks. I bet I'm a coyote or a fox. I'll ask Mary if I have a high-pitched howl."*

3. Concern for others: One of the features I like best about this game is the concern and encouragement the players show toward each other. Many players feel they haven't really finished the game until everyone else has guessed his

animal correctly. Many times I've seen six or seven players gathered around the last one, encouraging him on to the end.

An Optional Variation for older children. Listed below are starter questions that will help you narrow down the choice to a few animal groups (i.e., mammals, insects, mollusks, etc.). If you want to know more about the characteristics of individual animal groups, I recommend that you read a zoology text, or buy the inexpensive little booklet, *Zoology,* published by Golden Press, Inc., New York, NY 10022.

"Am I a vertebrate (animal with a backbone)?"

If the answer is yes, there are five possibilities: fishes, amphibians, reptiles, birds, mammals.

To divide the vertebrates into still smaller groups, ask if the animal is cold- or warm-blooded. "Cold-blooded vertebrate" means the animal's body temperature changes to match changes in the temperature of the surrounding environment. Cold-blooded vertebrates are: fishes, amphibians, reptiles.

"Warm-blooded vertebrate" means the animal maintains the same body temperature, regardless of whether it is cold or hot outside. The warm-blooded vertebrates are: birds and mammals.

If the answer is no (not a vertebrate animal), it means the animal is an *in*vertebrate (animal with no backbone). Here is a list of the more common invertebrates: *Annelids* (worms, leeches), *Echinoderms* (starfish, sand dollars), *Mollusks* (snails, clams), *Crustaceans* (crabs, crayfish), *Centipedes, Millipedes, Spiders, Insects.*

To divide the invertebrates into smaller categories, ask *"Do I have jointed legs?"* (Invertebrates with jointed legs are: *crustaceans, centipedes, millipedes, spiders, insects.* Invertebrates without jointed legs are: *annelids, echinoderms, mollusks.)*

Listed here are some questions that will help you narrow your choices even further: *Am I a predator? ... Can I swim? ... Can I fly? ... Do I live in the (ocean, desert, etc.)? ... Do I have (2, 4, 6, 8, or more than 8) legs? (Remember, you can ask only one question at a time!) ... Am I brightly colored? ... Am I active at night?*

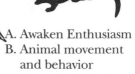

How come Noah only caught two fish ???

A. Awaken Enthusiasm
B. Animal movement and behavior
C. Day and night/ anywhere
D. 6 or more
E. 5 years and up
F. Index cards, pencils

THE IDEA is to find your mate amid the herd of cavorting beasts and birds on Noah's Ark. Begin by counting the number of players in your group, then make a list of animals half as long as the list of players. (Choose animals that have distinctive calls and/or movement, i.e., cranes, snakes, ducks, butterflies, frogs, and coyotes.)

Write the name of each animal on two 3 x 5 cards. When you finish there should be as many cards in your hand as there are players in the group—one card for each player. If you have an odd number of players, write the name of one of the animals on three cards, making a threesome to accommodate the extra player.

Have the players formed a large circle. Shuffle the cards and pass them out. Each child reads his card and becomes the animal whose name is on the card, keeping his identity a secret. Now collect the cards again.

On signal, the players all begin acting out the sounds, shapes, and typical movements of their animals, with the intention of attracting their mates. The action is hilarious when all the animals begin baying, croaking, screeching, whistling, strutting, flapping, leaping, and posing. They can make all the noise they want, but talking is prohibited—each animal must attract his mate solely by the authenticity of his behavior. The game ends in happy reunions and much laughter.

Noah's Ark

'Cause he only had two worms.

A. Awaken Enthusiasm
B. Animal characteris-
   tics, movement, and
   behavior
C. Day and night/
   anywhere
D. 3-6 in a group
E. 7 years and up
F. None

ANIMAL PARTS

ANIMAL PARTS works especially well for younger children and families. It's beautiful to see people of all ages enthusiastically playing together.

Divide your group into teams of four or five children each. Ask each team to select an animal they think is interesting. *Then* tell them that each group will have to imitate the body of their animal. The teams will have time to practice portraying their animal, before "performing" before the other teams who will try to guess the animal being imitated. (Encourage the teams to rely more on physical movement, rather than props or making the sounds of their animals.)

Give the groups about five minutes to work on their acts: *"Oh, no! A scorpion has eight legs—we'll all have to be legs! ... I can be the head, too, since I'm up front and my arms can be the pincers. ... Okay, I'll be the tail, but I don't think I can hold it too long. You guys will have to bend forward and hold onto each other to make the body. Ready?"*

Once everyone has finished practicing, have the groups, one at a time, share their animal. The other groups should wait until the "performing" group is completely finished before they call out what animal is being imitated.

Animal Parts

Animal Clue
Relay

A. Awaken Enthusiasm
B. Natural history, memory, teamwork
C. Day and night/ anywhere
D. 6 or more
E. 8 years and up
F. Animal clue cards, rope, pencils and paper

ANIMAL CLUE RELAY

makes learning exciting and gets everyone actively involved. It's a great beginning activity and can be used also to energize a group right after lunch, or in the late afternoon.

To start, make a large circle or square about 38 feet across. You are setting a boundary so that all the teams are equal distance (about 18 feet) from the center. You'll find rope is the most convenient way to make the boundary but you can use almost anything.

Have all the players divide into teams of three and give each team a pencil and a piece of paper. To add to the fun and create esprit de corps have each team choose a humorous nature name for itself. (For example, Waterfleas; Forget-Me-Nots; Tasmanian Devils; and Wandering Tattlers.) Now have the teams find a place on the outside perimeter of the circle. Then ask each team to introduce itself.

Place 30 animal clue cards face-up in the center of the circle. Explain to the players that there are six clue cards for each animal and that the object of the game is for each team to discover the identity of all five animals in the set.

(Explain that some of the clues are very general and therefore, by themselves, are difficult to pin to a specific animal. Other clues are more highly specific.) The teams do not have to find all six clue cards for each animal, but only enough of the clues to be sure of the animal's identity. Make sure to tell the players that the five animals are all distinct from each other and not closely related. For example, there wouldn't be a fox *and* a wolf in the same set.

To begin playing, each team sends one member at a time to fetch one clue card. The runners may not look at their clue card until they return to their waiting team members. As a group, the team reads the clue card and tries to guess the identity of the animal. A second player returns the card and selects a new one. A team may not have possession of more than one card at a time. The process continues until the team thinks it has identified all five animals.

When the teams have picked six or so cards, you can tell the runners they can look at the clue card to make sure it's a new one. Towards the end of the game, you can help the teams still playing, by telling the runners they can pick two cards at a time.

When a team thinks it knows the identity of all five animals, it should report to the referee and show its answers. (Caution: Some teams may try to guess too quickly. It is important to remind the players to acquire enough clues and information to be reasonably sure of the identity of each animal. Often the team who finishes first gets the lowest score!)

Since people tend to enjoy the things they do success-fully, I like to use the following scoring system because it handsomely rewards everyone's efforts. The players see through the generous grading, but nevertheless, are quite delighted with their high scores.

Give one point for every correct guess, and two points off for every incorrect guess. Then assign nine points for each guess a team makes, up to five guesses. The first team to finish gets three extra points; the second place team gets two extra points; and any team that finishes gets one extra point. Then multiply the total points by two.

Let's say the Wandering Tattlers correctly guess the identity of four of the animals. Tell them: *"You get four points for the correct guesses, plus one point for finishing the game."* (The team didn't place first or second.) *"And you guessed five times, so five times nine is forty-five. Forty-five points plus four and one equals fifty. Take off two points for the incorrect guess and you have forty-eight. Now we'll multiply this by two and you have ..... ninety-six points. Great job Wandering Tattlers!"*

Below are sample clues for five ocean animals that you can use in creating your own game. Or, if you prefer, you can order beautifully designed sets of animal clue cards for the rainforest and ocean environments from Dawn Publications. Each set contains 60 animal clue cards and pictures of ten animals (See page 175).

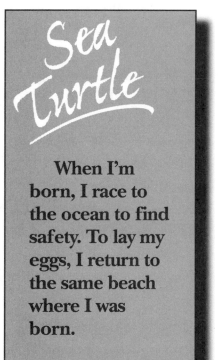

Sea Turtle

When I'm born, I race to the ocean to find safety. To lay my eggs, I return to the same beach where I was born.

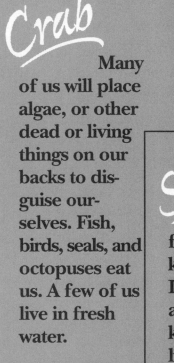

Crab

Many of us will place algae, or other dead or living things on our backs to disguise ourselves. Fish, birds, seals, and octopuses eat us. A few of us live in fresh water.

Shark

I have fins. I have to keep swimming or I sink. I don't have an air bladder that keeps me afloat, like fish do. That's why you'll always see me cruising around. (Some people think I am a fish, but I'm not!)

Star Fish

I open a shell and move part of my stomach into the shell. Then I pour juices into the shell to help me eat. My colors are red, orange, and yellow.

Whale

When I'm a baby I weigh seven tons and I'm about 24 feet long. I gain 200 pounds every day! That's nine pounds an hour. As an adult, I may eat three tons of food every day. I eat a shrimp-like animal called krill.

PLAY AND DISCOVERY

The games shared here are filled with hilarity, suspense and adventure, and are indeed great fun. I believe that nature games are a fine stepping stone to lead the child into a deeper appreciation of the natural world. My greatest concern is that children have joyous first experiences with the natural world. This way, their associations with the natural world begin on a happy note, and will always be fond ones.

In spirit, these games are like those played by Indian boys in the prairie days: stalking animals and "enemies"; moving soundlessly; learning to be unseen even by wary eyes; training ears to catch and recognize every sound, eyes to miss not a single detail; and practicing quickness of foot and agility of movement. The games of the Indian boy became the survival skills of the hunter, providing food and bringing him into intimate communion with the land on which he lived and the creatures among whom he walked.

Catch the Horse

AT THE Aullwood Audubon Nature Center in Dayton, Ohio, there is an eight-acre prairie of grass 8 to 10 feet high. When I worked there, we sectioned off a small portion for games involving exploring, hiding, and running. On that magnificent little piece of prairie we played **Catch the Horse** in grand fashion.

"In pioneer times," we told the children, *"the settlers would often lose their horses in the prairie, and so someone would have to climb a tree to try and spot them. The person in the tree would wave directions to those chasing the horse."* At the Audubon Center we stationed a child in a tree, with a big red bandanna for signaling. The horse took his head start, then the search began. The horse would be spotted many times, but would usually escape before the searchers could close in. The lookout would then give new directions, and the children would once more go off in hot pursuit.

The children enjoyed playing in the prairie so much that they reacted with indignation whenever we told them that it would have to be burned. (The Audubon Society set fire to the prairie every two years to prevent it from turning into a forest.) Again and again, I've seen that if people have a positive, joyful first encounter with some

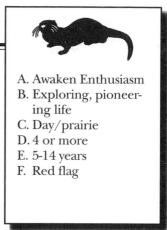

A. Awaken Enthusiasm
B. Exploring, pioneer-
   ing life
C. Day/prairie
D. 4 or more
E. 5-14 years
F. Red flag

aspect of nature, they will become protective toward that life form or environment.

Cornfields and tall-grass prairies are ideal sites for this game. Choose from the group the one member (possibly an adult) who has the best agility and endurance—he will be the "horse." While everyone else closes their eyes, the horse takes a three-minute head start. When time is up, everyone begins hunting through the brush to try and flush out the horse. Whoever spots him first calls to the others to join the chase.

I especially remember playing horse for a third-grade class, dodging their charges and lunges for a good fifteen or twenty minutes. Several times their teacher organized them for circling maneuvers, but each time I was just barely able to slip through the closing net. In the end we were all complete-ly exhausted from crashing through the ten-foot grass. The momentum of countless circles I'd run around the children flung me dizzily to the Earth, and as I turned over on my back the children piled on top of me. Their diving forms, the grass and the trees, the liquid sky all appeared to revolve overhead in vast, sweeping circles. We lay there totally spent, but savoring an awesome state of oneness with the prairie.

A. Focus Attention
B. Calmness, observa-
   tion
C. Night/road or trail
D. 4 or more
E. 7 years and up
F. Flashlights

Camouflage

A GOOD TIME to play **Camouflage** is on the way home from a night hike; but you can also play it on those wonderful summer evenings when dusk is just turning to nightfall.

Divide the group into two teams, hiders and searchers. The hiders scatter along a designated section of trail. How close to the trail they will hide depends on the brightness of the moon and whether or not the searchers have flashlights. Since each hider's whole body must be in full view from at least one point along the trail, they will have to try to blend with the profiles of natural objects around them to remain unseen.

The American Indian hunter, who sometimes donned camouflage costume for the purpose, also tried to think like and enter into the consciousness of the animal or object he was impersonating. He knew that the deer, bear or bird he hunted could detect his presence not just with its eyes, nose, and ears, but with an ability to "sense" a man's presence. The hiders can try to tune in to this intuitive faculty, which we humans also have, by trying to feel that they are a natural part of the objects around them; and the searchers can try to sense a foreign presence among the rocks and leaves. As soon as all the searchers pass by him (they should travel close together), each hider can reveal himself.

A. Awaken Enthusiasm
B. Exploring, intense
   alertness, stalking
C. Day/thicket, forest
D. 13 or more
E. 9 years and up
F. Beans, noisemakers

BRAVE YOUNG adventurers make their way to safety through a forest infested with wildmen. Find a bushy, tangly area seamed with trails, or any terrain with good cover. A thick woods is ideal (if free of poison oak or poison ivy!). You will need to mark out the boundaries of your "wild-man woods." The size of the area depends on how many people are playing and how good the cover is. If the terrain is more open than thick woods, or if you have a large group, you'll want to broaden the boundaries.

Pick five to eight adults or older children to act as wildmen. They should dress to fit their ferocious roles, applying mud and ketchup for gory effect and equipping themselves with a variety of noisemakers. The wildmen scatter through the thicket ready to catch—or at least liven things up for—anyone they meet.

Before entering the woods, each child is given four beans. Each time he is caught, the wildman demands one of his beans. He must duly turn over the bean and return

Wildmen
in the Alders

to the starting line to try again. If he loses all his beans, it is all right to give him more. Players returning to the start should go around the outside of the playing area, to avoid confusing the wildmen.

How much fun the children have depends largely on the attitude of the wildmen. Instead of collecting as many beans as they can, the wildmen should try to give the other children a good time: providing close escapes by coming within an inch of catching someone, then tripping on a root with a loud cry of dismay. The wildmen can set traps for the faster children, while somehow letting the slower ones slip by. Emphasize also to the wildmen the importance of safety, and not to scare the children so much that they run too fast and out-of-control in steep or brushy areas. You should also go over the play area very carefully beforehand to make sure there aren't any potential hazards like poison oak, hornet's nests, large holes, and steep slopes.

When the children are assembled and ready, call out to the wildmen to *"make some noise and let us know if you're in there."* The ensuing din of duck calls, whistles, bugles, tin pans and screechings, orchestrated into one grand horrible noise, will add greatly to the excitement of entering the forest. Children love a good scare and will talk about it for days afterwards.

Sleeping Miser

CHOOSE ONE PERSON in your group to be the **Sleeping Miser.** The rest of the group will be stalkers. The miser sits blindfolded on the ground, jealously guarding an object of great value that rests in front of him. (You can use a hat or a flag.) But a miser can't stay awake forever guarding his treasure, and he has fallen asleep.

Look for an area where stalkers will make some, but not a lot of noise. The stalkers form a ring around the miser, about 25 feet away (you can reduce the distance if there is noisy ground cover). At a signal, the stalkers begin to advance as quietly as possible (encourage them to go barefoot if they wish). They must try to get close enough

A. Focus Attention
B. Calmness, concentration, stalking
C. Day/clearing
D. 5 or more
E. 6 years and up
F. One blindfold

to touch the treasure without waking up the miser; so they will need to be aware and in control of every movement of their bodies. If the miser clearly hears an approaching stalker, he points in that direction. The referee, standing behind the sleeping miser, seconds the miser's point if the noise made was significant. Anyone pointed out by the referee must freeze. (Tell the miser and players that the referee will be pointing out only the louder noises and may not second every point of the miser.)

When a number of stalkers have been frozen or have touched the treasure, stop the game and allow the frozen ones to go back to the perimeter and start over. At the same time, let those who have touched the treasure walk to the perimeter to wait quietly until the game is over. Make sure no one advances under the cover of the time-out noises. On signal, everyone again begins sneaking up on the miser. Allow no running or diving for the treasure. The stalker who succeeds in first touching the treasure is Miser for the next game.

Because everyone is very quiet during **Sleeping Miser,** there is a good chance of seeing the more secretive animals if you are in a wild place. This is also a good game for teaching self-control and calming down a too-rambunctious group of children, and preparing them for more quiet activities.

A. Awaken Enthusiasm
B. Auditory awareness,
   concentration
C. Day/clearing or
   road
D. 6 or more
E. 5 years and up
F. One blindfold

Bat & Moth

HAVE THE GROUP form a circle 10-15 feet across. Choose a member of the circle to be the bat, then have him come to the center of the circle to be blindfolded. Designate three to five other children as moths and ask them also to come to the center of the circle. The bat tries to catch the moths.

Whenever the bat calls out *"Bat!"* the moths call back *"Moth!"* Tell the moths: *"Every time you hear the bat call out 'Bat!' it's his sonar signal hitting you. He sends it out to see if there's anything out there. His cry bounces off you and returns to him like a sonar signal. The return signal is the word 'Moth!' that you shout. Now he knows moths are near— and he's ready to eat!"*

The bat tracks down and tags the moths by listening to their responses. (Encourage the bat to tag around waist high.) It takes concentration, confidence, and the ability to move well to be a successful bat. Try to choose a player with these characteristics so that the game will be more dynamic and fun. If it's necessary to help the bat out, you can make the circle smaller: *"Okay, everyone take a deer's step forward."* Use this ploy if the bat is too timid, or after several moths have been caught. Another tip for tracking the moths more easily is to shout bat more frequently, for example, *"Bat...bat...bat,"* instead of, *"Bat......... bat........bat."*

Bat and Moth also teaches scientific concepts like adaptation, natural selection, and predator-prey, as well as listening and concentration. After all the moths have been caught, ask if anyone noticed any characteristic that any of the moths had that helped them to survive longer. Examples could be that the moth was fast, stooped low to the ground, or had a quiet voice. Remind the players that these successful traits help the individual moth to live longer, and this process is called natural selection.

Children love **Bat and Moth**, and my only challenge while playing it is that the children sometimes don't want to do anything else!

Thinis game is played on a untravelled, unpaved road or dirt driveway at night. The watcher sits in the middle of the road, with his eyes closed and a flashlight in hand. The children line up at a starting point 15 feet away. Then several children try to stalk past him together and reach home base, a line 10 feet beyond. If the watcher hears anything, he shines his light in that direction. Anyone the light touches must freeze. (No fair sweeping the light around!) After several players have been frozen, call a time out to let them return to the start and try again. The first to pass the watcher and reach home base becomes the new *Watcher of the Road*.

A. Focus Attention
B. Calmness, concen-
tration, stalking
C. Night/road
D. 5 or more
E. 5-13 years
F. One flashlight

*Watcher
of the
Road*

SPOTTING AND ATTRACTING ANIMALS

Almost everyone loves to watch animals. I feel this is so because animals exemplify to us so perfectly the qualities of purity and spontaneity; they are a constant reminder that all creatures— including ourselves—have a right to a free and contented life.

I remember an experience I had as a boy that awakened in me a life-long fascination for marshes, and for a life lived wild and free. I was out playing alone on a cold, foggy morning when suddenly I heard a startling chorus of "whouks" coming toward me through the air. I peered intently at the thick fog, hoping for at least a glimpse of the geese. Seconds passed; the tempo of their cries increased. They were going to fly directly overhead! I could hear their wings slapping just yards above me. All of a sudden,

SECTION
6

bursting through a gap in the fog, came a large flock of pearl-white snow geese. It was as if the sky had given birth to them. For five or six wonderful seconds their sleek and graceful forms were visible, then they merged once again into the fog. Their fading calls seemed to say "follow us—follow us." When I grew older, I did follow and live with them.

I live in the forest now, where I seldom see geese. But when they do fly overhead, their calls always tempt me to follow them again.

Children are especially aware of their kinship with animals. (Their pets, stuffed bears, and animal books and pictures testify to this.) Any child will tell you that the most important part of a nature outing is seeing wild animals. The games in this chapter are designed to teach children simple and well-tested methods for attracting animals.

Bird Calling

BIRD WATCHERS ("birders") have traditionally been thought of as eccentric types who trudge about the woods and climb trees with unruly collections of notebooks, binoculars and cameras. But if you ever get a chance to observe birds closely, you'll discover that they're beautiful to see and listen to, and utterly fascinating in their habits. You may find yourself not only understanding the birders' obsession, but catching it yourself!

In the bird world you'll find exquisite beauty and almost unimaginable homeliness; perfect grace and total clumsiness; fearsome power and gentle humility; silent soaring in rarified heights, and earthy cackling and squabbling.

A. Direct Experience
B. Attracting birds,
   empathy, patience
C. Day and night/
   thicket, forest
D. 1 or more
E. 4 years and up
F. None

THERE IS A BIRD CALL that you can easily do with no more equipment than your own mouth. It attracts many of the smaller species: sparrows, warblers, jays, vireos, chickadees, nuthatches, hummingbirds, flycatchers, bushtits, orioles, kinglets, wrens, and others. In the following section on predator calls, you will learn to attract some of the larger birds.

The call consists of a series of rhythmically-repeated "psssh" sounds. Different rhythms work with different birds. Here are a couple of simple rhythms you can start with:

pssh ...... pssh ...... pssh ......

pssh ..... pssh ..... pssh-pssh ..... pssh ..... pssh

Each of these series should last about three seconds. Experiment to find the rhythms that work best for the birds in your area.

For the best results when you use this call, wait until you hear birds nearby, then kneel or stand motionless by shrubs or trees that will partially hide you and give the birds something to land on. Begin calling the series, pausing after three or four rounds to listen for the incoming birds.

The birds will respond quickly if they are going to respond at all. Some birds, like rufous-sided towhees, will fly to the nearest lookout post to find out what is going on. Others, like the wrentit, will slowly, warily come closer. When the birds have come near, a single series or a couple of notes may be all you'll need to keep them nearby. I think the reason this call works is that the "psssh" sound resembles many birds' scolding call. (Some naturalists believe it sounds like a mother bird's feeding call to her young; others, that it merely provokes the birds' curiosity.)

Smaller birds dislike the presence of predators and will frequently mob a hawk or owl in hopes of driving it away. While hiking high in the Sierras, a group of Boy Scouts and I experienced a dramatic case of bird-mobbing. We were in the middle of a low-growing alder thicket when a pine marten scampered into view just eight feet away. (Pine martens are related to the weasels and are about the size of a small domestic cat. They are agile climbers and snatch birds as part of their diet.)

We gave our "distress call," and in no more than a minute ten eager birds had gathered to rescue us. They landed very close to the marten, scolding him fervently and indignantly until he decided to move on.

Children enjoy using this call. Many times I've been with groups of children who lay silently on the forest floor, completely absorbed in watching the birds that flew in overhead coming in to answer the children's signals.

Using an audio recording of a screech owl will give you even better results. (Screech owls are small owls who sometimes eat small birds.) Many times while using this owl recording I've had 50 to 75 birds flock in and begin singing all around me. I like to alternate the calls—first playing the owl recording, then saying a few pssshes, then again playing the screech owl, etc. Because the screech owl call is so effective, it's important that you avoid using it during the breeding season.

In *A Sharing Nature Walk,* the audio companion cassette to this book, there's a recording of a screech owl to be used with this activity (see page 174).

Birds on

THE INSPIRATION for this activity came from a statement I read or heard many years ago: "There are two kinds of birders. The first kind study birds at a distance, recording their physical characteristics and behavior. The others are on more intimate terms with the birds; in fact, birds like them as much as they do other birds, and will even land on them to get as close to them as possible."

Not having Saint Francis' way with birds, but desiring a deeper rapport with the bird family, I wondered: would birds come to me if I added a few props to my bird-watching strategy? I'd used the "psssh" call (see Bird Calling activity, page 116) for years, and had had birds almost land on my head. What would happen if I covered myself with a blanket and held a stick? Would birds land on the stick?

Not long ago I grabbed an old green blanket and an eight-foot branch and wandered through the forest until I heard bird calls. Sitting down and wrapping the blanket around me like a hooded robe, I held the stick motionless in the air and began making the "psssh" call. Immediately I heard approaching "aank-aank-aanks" and braced myself for the arrival of red-breasted nuthatches. (Red-breasted nuthatches look somewhat like miniature woodpeckers.)

Out of the highest tree branches came two curious nuthatches. They paused to look around, so I called again, and one swooped down and landed on the tip of the branch I was holding. He began working his way down the

a Stick

A. Direct Experience
B. Attracting birds, empathy, patience
C. Day and night/ thicket, forest
D. 1-3 per group
E. 7 years and up
F. Drab blanket, stick

branch until he was less than two feet from me, where he stared intently at my shadowed face. Meanwhile, the other nuthatch made the first of four trips from the nearest tree branch to my stick.

These are some suggestions and considerations we've found important for success with **Bird on a Stick**: *1) Birds are most active in the morning. 2) Birds are less likely to shy away from drab-colored blankets and sheets. (Remember to cover your face with shadows cast by the blanket.) 3) Birds are more likely to approach you in a thicket or forest, where your presence is less obtrusive. 4) Choose a place where you can hear sounds of bird activity. 5) Position yourself in a small clearing, so that the birds will have no other place to land but on your stick. 6) Hold the stick motionless. (Younger children can hold onto a young tree as their stick.)*

Calling Predators

PREDATORS ARE very wary creatures. You'll rarely see foxes, bobcats, mountain lions, hawks or eagles unless you have the good fortune to stumble upon or successfully track down a nest or den site. But their impressive wild beauty and rarity make it all the more exciting when you do see them. You can buy a predator call for about twelve dollars at a sporting goods store, and with it draw these animals to you. The call imitates the sound of wounded rabbit and often attracts curious non-predators as well; curious deer may come around for a look.

Find an area with signs of heavy animal activity (game trails and animal droppings, for example). Hide yourself in a thicket or other natural cover with a clearing around it. The reason for the clearing is so you'll see the approaching animal long before he sees you. A group of college students ignored this precaution once and had a good scare when a fox jumped right in among them!

To use the predator call, hold the middle of it between your thumb and index finger while enclosing the rest of the call with your other fingers. The little finger should close over the end. For the first third of the call, keep your little finger over the end to suppress the noise; then release the little finger, ring, and middle fingers to achieve a wailing sound. Do this in one smooth sequence.

A. Direct Experience
B. Attracting predators, overcoming fears, patience
C. Dawn, dusk, night/ areas with cover
D. 1 or more
E. 7 years and up
F. Predator call

It should make a scream or cry not unlike a baby's wail.

You want as many animals as possible to hear the call, but you also want to produce a realistic effect as the animals come closer; so give a couple of very loud series of calls to attract their attention, then gradually lower the volume until the calls are only a whimper. Keep a watchful eye out, because a fox could be sneaking toward you.

Predator-calling doesn't work every time, but the results can be spectacular. A scout group and I once watched a bobcat slither to within 60 feet of us. Another time, a buck responded to the call by running up and snorting at me. And I was with another scout group when a goshawk, a large hawk that sometimes runs on the ground to catch its prey, screamed over our heads like a bullet. We then spotted a red-tail hawk circling overhead, so we forgot all about the goshawk. Little did we know that he had landed quietly and was stalking us from behind; one of the scouts moved suddenly and startled the goshawk into flight, just 35 feet behind us.

Children generally stay quiet and attentive during the half-hour I allow for calling. Even if no predators or deer come close, they enjoy the suspense and the silence of the forest, the scuffling of the squirrels, and the many bird calls.

A. Focus Attention
B. Stalking, wildlife observation
C. Dawn, dusk, night/anywhere
D. 1 or more
E. 7 years and up
F. None

Recon-Hike

AFTER PREPARING for the hike, create an atmosphere of suspense that the children will enjoy, by addressing the group in a serious, conspiratorial tone: "*We are about to undertake a special mission. Our objective is to search the surrounding area thoroughly, missing nothing. We are to observe and remember all the terrain and life-forms who live there. There have been signs of recent predator activity in this area, so it is important that we remain hidden and unseen.*"

These are the suggested preparations for the **Recon-Hike:** 1) Wear only non-rustling clothing like wool or cotton. 2) Camouflage yourself by wearing colors that match the colors of the area. 3) Darken your face and hands. 4) Put on quiet walking shoes or go barefoot.

Guidelines to follow during the hike: 1) Always try to stay under or near cover. 2) Move slowly, pausing every few steps to look around. 3) Avoid walking in the same direction as the wind is blowing, so your scent won't be carried ahead of you.

Camouflaged reconnaissance increases a child's awareness of his environment and strengthens his ability to describe what he sees. Because the children are very quiet and watchful, there is a good chance of seeing wildlife. I recall a group of four boys at a sixth grade environmental education camp who would do virtually anything to see wild animals. In fact, this game was born of the inspiration of their enthusiasm.

The first day at camp, these four boys asked me how they could see more animals. Because they were also interested in Indians, I told them that Indian hunters used to fast for several days to reduce their body scent, so that the animals they hunted couldn't smell them. I never dreamed that the boys would take my offhand comment seriously, much less that they would take it even further, I believe, than any Indian ever did.

The next day while we were swimming, one of the boys got stuck up to his hips in a sea of gooey clay. We all pitched in to help him out, and of course before long you could hardly tell us apart. One of the boys, thoroughly plastered with clay, jubilantly announced that the animals could now neither smell nor see us, because the mud covered up our human scent and camouflaged our bodies as well.

Perfecting our disguises with generous dollops of clay, we headed warily for cover and then stalked the woods in search of animals. It was midday, so most of the animals were inactive and hidden from sight; still, we had great fun: we would spot a promising clearing, then divide up and surround it. On signal, five brown mud-caked forms would pop up from behind rocks, trees, and grass-clumps, gazing intently for any movements.

After an hour or so, the caked mud began to itch horribly; we hurried back toward the camp to wash up. Just as we entered the walkway to the main building, an excited teacher met us. The Board of Education had just arrived to tour the camp and were—at that very moment—just inside the door. No matter how badly we itched, we would simply have to wait out in the woods until they left. Our wait was sheer agony, but was relieved by many peals of boyish laughter.

Journey to the Heart of Nature

My young friend Katy, returning from a week of wilderness camp, enthusiastically told me about all the rock climbing, hiking, and boating she had done. "What did you enjoy most?" I asked. Katy's reply was striking for its simplicity: "When I spent time alone in nature."

Being alone outdoors is a powerful and healing experience for young people. There, they are in direct contact with the rocks and trees. Nature Herself becomes their teacher. It is rewarding to see young people become so absorbed in experiencing nature. I enjoy, too, the creative spirit that a nature

experience seems to evoke, reflected in the descriptive names the children give to their special places—names like Serenity Cove, Faraway View, and Shimmering Leaf Glade. Because the experience of solitude in nature is so powerful, my friend Michael Deranja and I wrote Journey to the Heart of Nature, A Guided Exploration. *The book guides participants in selecting and exploring their own special place in nature in a series of five visits. A variety of stories and activities guide the "adventurers" so their time is focused and meaningful. Learning to love and care for nature in one place will encourage a love for all of nature.*

The following three activities give a taste of a journey into the heart of nature, and can serve as a wonderful introduction to this Earth Stewardship program.

Exploring Special Places

(A Set of Four Related Activities)

SELECT a natural area with a variety of habitats where the group can spread out and each person can find a special place. If you have younger children you'll want to look for an area with a natural boundary so you can keep everyone in sight. If the area is safe, it may be appropriate for young adults to go farther afield if they are knowledgeable about the outdoors.

A. Direct Experience
B. Exploration, reflection
C. Day/Natural area with varied habitats
D. 2 or more
E. 10 years and up
F. An Explorer's Guide for each child (see reproducible pages 128 to 133), pencils, clip boards, invitation cards

Tell the group that they will have a certain amount of time (25 to 40 minutes is a good range) to find a special place and to do activities from the **Explorer's Guide**. They do not have to do every activity, but should choose the ones that most interest them and give the greatest sense of involvement with their special place. They will also make an invitation card to invite a guest to their special place. At the specified time, the explorers are to come back and divide into pairs and share their places (it takes about 20 minutes). Afterwards, they meet together again and share their discoveries with the rest of the group.

Finding and Exploring Special Places
Explorer's Guide Activities—35 Minutes*
Sharing Your Site with a Friend—20 Minutes
Group Sharing—15 Minutes

Pass out pencils, writing boards, and the **Explorer's Guide** and explain some of its activities with enthusiasm so that the children can begin to catch the spirit of the adventure. For example, tell the explorers if they sketch their best view, they can give it to their guest to see if he can find it by using the drawing as a guide.

Designate the area where everyone is to search for a special place, and make arrangements for everyone to return at the same time. Tell them you will be walking around to see where everyone is and how they are doing.

* Choose a time that is appropriate for the group. Also allow time for transition between the activities. The activities can be done individually if the group has a short attention span and requires more guidance.

MY JOURNEY TO:

EXPLORER: _____

First Impressions

AFTER CHOOSING a special area, take time to wander around and just have fun. Then pick a comfortable spot where you can think about your place and answer these questions.

WHAT ARE some of the first things you noticed about your site?

_____

_____

_____

_____

_____

_____

_____

HOW DO YOU FEEL being here?

_____

_____

_____

_____

_____

_____

_____

PICK A NAME that suits your special place. You can change it later, if you think of something better. But naming it at the start will help you make it your own right away.

THE NAME OF MY
SPECIAL PLACE IS _____

A. FIND the best view and give it a special name. Then sketch the view in this "photo" space. Later, you'll see if a friend can find your "best" view by using your drawing as a guide.

B. FIND the best place to listen for nature sounds. Then, see how long it takes to hear at least five different natural sounds. See if you can figure out what is making the sounds.

WRITE DOWN THE SOUNDS (AND WHO MADE THEM):

1) _____

2) _____

3) _____

4) _____

5) _____

C. DESCRIBE a bird's call or any other natural sound that you hear, using words or letters. For example, the gathering call of the California Quail has been described as "Chi-*ca*-go!" or "Come-*right*-here!" and the sound of a seal as "Arhk, Arhk."

THE SOUND YOU HEARD: _____

D. FIND the oldest or
most striking tree. Draw the
tree and tell why it's unique.

E. USE YOUR HANDS to find the warmest and
coldest places. Also look for the wettest and driest sites.
Can you find the windiest and calmest places? Make a
simple map of your area and mark all these places on it.

F. STOP AT DIFFERENT places. Close your eyes and
focus your attention on the sense of smell. Find three
different smells and describe them. See if you can figure
out where they come from.

1) _____

2) _____

3) _____

G. FIND something that:

1) IS SMALL AND HAS FIVE OR MORE COLORS

2) MAKES YOU SMILE

Writing a poem is another way to become more aware of your site. Choose a favorite place and sit for a few minutes watching and enjoying. Notice how each sound, movement, texture and color is different. Feel the special quality that each thing expresses. If you see a darting, swift-moving flock of birds, feel in your heart the joy of their flight. If you see a tree swaying in a light breeze, feel its strength and gracefulness. Try writing a Vertical Poem—you'll be surprised how easy it is.

Vertical Poem

Choose a word that captures the feeling of the place you've chosen. Then use each letter of the word to begin a line of your poem. While walking on Mount Subasio near Assisi, Italy, I wrote a poem to the word "spring." The flower-covered hillsides expressed a feeling of excitement as the shadows of the clouds raced over them.

S UN-MADE CLOUD SHADOWS

P LACED ON THE EARTH

R UNNING ACROSS ITS SURFACE

I N AND OUT OF THE SUN I SIT

N OT LONG DOES THE CLOUD'S TWIN STAY

G OING, GOING ON ITS WAY.

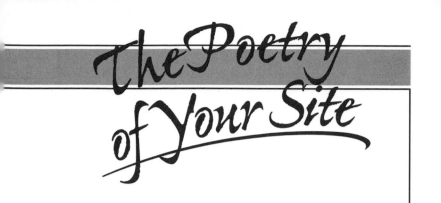

The Poetry of Your Site

Now write the word you've chosen, with one letter on each line. Then use each letter to begin a line of your poem.

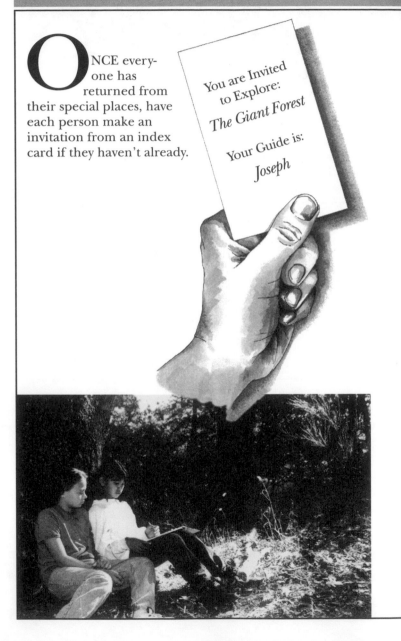

ONCE everyone has returned from their special places, have each person make an invitation from an index card if they haven't already.

You are Invited to Explore:
The Giant Forest

Your Guide is:
Joseph

Sharing Your Site with a Friend

Ask half the group to put their cards into a hat; then have those still holding cards draw a card out of the hat. Once they've picked a card, they should pair up with the person whose card they've drawn. Then, for example, if Mary picks Barbara's card, Mary keeps Barbara's card and gives her own to Barbara. Then Barbara and Mary go off to share their special places with each other. Have the pairs share the activities they've done, as well as anything else they've discovered about their special places.

Once the pairs are finished sharing, gather together and go over the activities, one at a time, allowing people to share their place names, sketches, poems, etc., with the rest of the group. I like to start the sharing by having everyone point in the direction of their special place. There's always much laughter when the children extend their arms pointing in all directions.

The activities in Section 7 comprise just a small part of the Earth Stewardship program presented in *Journey to the Heart of Nature* (see page 174). Themes for visits to a special place include: One Big Family, Getting Close to Nature, and Caring for Your Site. Activities and inspiring stories help the participants feel a sense of belonging and connection with their site. In addition to the book, a set of activity masters is also available to support teachers of these Earth Stewardship activities. See page 174 for more information.

ADVENTURES

By protecting ourselves from weather and soil, bugs and animals, many of us have denied ourselves the vitality and sense of well-being that come from living attuned to natural cycles and events. Our natural instinct for self-protection needs balancing by an adventuresome spirit. A spirit of reaching out to touch and explore the world places us where nature can easily display her powers before us.

At some time during my education as a naturalist, I read or heard that certain California Indians used to hunt ducks by wading in the marshes at night. Under cover of darkness they walked right up to the ducks. As a bird watcher, I was intrigued by the possibilities—I was eager to try observing waterfowl while immersed in their native element.

One evening I put on old pants and shoes and walked out to my favorite marsh. As I neared the marsh around dusk, I was startled by a thunderous roar. Thousands of geese trembled together in a huge flock, flapping hard to build momentum for their takeoff... then erupted, covering the sky with their bodies. Skimming ahead over the cattails were countless flocks of ducks, criss-crossing in every direction.

I hurried into the water, oblivious of its wintry cold because of my awareness of the intense energy of the marsh, vibrating through the forms of fast-flying ducks and V-shaped strings of clamoring geese. When the moonless night fell and blended my presence into its darkness, the ducks began flying extremely close. Whirs, waffles, and whistles passed by my ears—exhilarating!—and ducks were alighting all around me like big splashing raindrops.

Suddenly I sensed a presence overhead and looked up; hovering there above me was a great horned owl. With only my head out of the water, she couldn't decide whether I was fit prey or not. Meanwhile, ducks were paddling all around me, many coming so close I could have reached out and touched them. Later, when I was standing motionless in shallower water, one little duck swam unconcernedly between my legs.

The whole experience was so magical that I completely forgot myself and the cold. I spent two or three hours wading silently from one duck-inhabited pothole to another, using my hands and ears to guide me through the night blackness.

It is very helpful—almost essential—for people at first to have startling, captivating experiences in nature. This kind of first contact extinguishes for a moment the self-enclosing preoccupations and worries that keep us from feeling our identity with other expressions of life. From that release into expanded awareness and concern, love naturally follows. And memories of moments of love and expansion act as reminders of, and incentives to, a more sensitive way of living.

Still-Hunting

STILL-HUNTING was practiced by the American Indians. A brave who wanted to still-hunt would go to a place he knew well and felt attracted to. There, in the forest or on a hillside, he would sit down and let his mind settle into a still and watchful mood. If his arrival had caused a disturbance among the creatures around him, he waited patiently until the world of nature

A. Direct Experience
B. Serenity, spotting wildlife
C. Day and night/ anywhere
D. 1 or more
E. 7 years and up
F. None

returned to its normal, harmonious routine. Usually, his only desire in still-hunting was to observe and learn.

When you go still-hunting, let your sitting-place choose you. You may be intuitively guided to a specific place in order to learn a certain lesson. For the first part of your stay, remain motionless, not even turning your head. Be as unobtrusive as you can, letting the world around you go on as it does when you aren't there. Feel that you are part of the natural surroundings; mentally move with the shimmering leaves, or dance with the butterfly as it darts and dodges through the air. Because you are still, curious animals may come close for a look at you. I was once approached from behind by a mysterious animal that made strange p-thumping noises as it moved. When the beast had come to within about seven feet, my courage flagged and I quickly turned my head. Off into the bushes fled that vicious predator, the cotton-tail rabbit!

Sharing private experiences with friends after a still-hunt brings a group closer together. Each still-hunter can tell about a plant or animal he has seen, and the qualities he felt it exemplified. Another good way to share still-hunting experiences is for each child to act out for the others something he saw, or a feeling he had, while sitting. The others try to tune in to the deeper mood of what he is saying. The tone of these sharing times should always be respectful and sensitive, if real communication of feelings and experiences is to happen.

Evening is a wonderful time to be outdoors. Many animals are active and easily seen. The day's last light gives everything a rich, golden color that some call "glory light," and the western sky fills with great beauty. Then, as our sun leaves us, we see other stars—just a few at first, then thousands.

The *Sunset Watch* activity helps you to notice and enjoy the exciting events that happen around sundown. Below is a list of things you might observe. What you see will depend on the area and time of year. Mark each event in the order it happens. For example, if you first notice that the day birds are quiet, you would write number "1" next to *day birds*. If you hear an owl or other night bird a little later, write number "2" for *owl calling*, and so on. If an event is continually changing, like the clouds turning color, you can note the changes by writing more than one number for the event—for example, "5" and "8" *clouds change color*.

Besides watching the sun set in the western sky, look in all the other directions. Don't worry about missing something or getting the order exactly as things happen. Just put a number by the things you see when you see them.

A. Direct Experience
B. Astronomy, wildlife biology, serenity
C. Sunset or sunrise
D. 1 or more
E. 9 years and up
F. Worksheets (see next page), pencils, flashlight

Because each location is unique, you'll probably see other events as well. You might see a flock of birds gathering in a tree, for example, or a mammal beginning its evening ramble, fish jumping for flying insects, or frogs singing. When you see anything special, write it down under *other events.* Write a number for each of these events so you have a record of when it occurred.

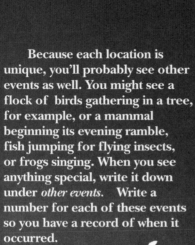

For the best viewing, try to arrive at your sunset viewpoint 15 minutes before actual sundown and plan to stay for about an hour after the sun sets. Arriving only 15 minutes beforehand is especially important if you are leading a group, because then they won't have to wait too long before the dramatic changes in lighting and animal activity begin. Remember to bring a flashlight with you so you can stay as long as you want.

Following, are some thought provoking facts you may want to read and share with others during a **Sunset Watch**:

Would you believe that most of us can see better than a bear at

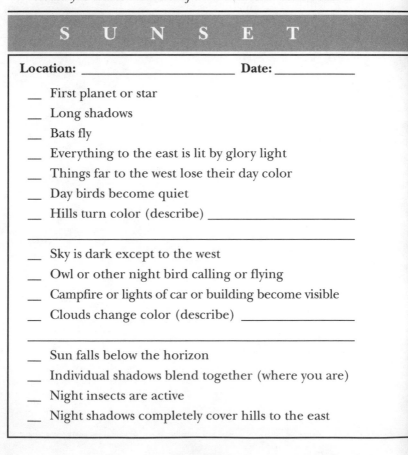

S U N S E T

Location: _____ **Date:** _____

__ First planet or star
__ Long shadows
__ Bats fly
__ Everything to the east is lit by glory light
__ Things far to the west lose their day color
__ Day birds become quiet
__ Hills turn color (describe) _____

__ Sky is dark except to the west
__ Owl or other night bird calling or flying
__ Campfire or lights of car or building become visible
__ Clouds change color (describe) _____

__ Sun falls below the horizon
__ Individual shadows blend together (where you are)
__ Night insects are active
__ Night shadows completely cover hills to the east

night, and almost as well as a cat? Our night vision seldom reaches full power, because we're usually surrounded by artificial light. It takes our eyes 45 minutes to recover their full night vision after looking into strong light.

On a clear, dark night you're likely to see about two thousand stars—out of the one billion billion stars that are known to exist.

Light travels at 186,000 miles a second. Yet some stars are so far away that it takes hundreds, thousands, or even millions of years for their light to reach us. When you look at a star, you may be seeing light that began its long journey hundreds of years ago.

W   A   T   C   H

___ Sky turns a soft pink or violet color (after sundown)

___ Moon appears or brightens

___ Clouds no longer visible

___ North Star and Little Dipper or Southern Cross appear

___ Temperature cools

___ Wind speed or direction changes

___ First shooting star or meteor

Other Events: Record and number any other events you noticed—for example, perhaps you saw a satellite or heard a wolf or coyote.

_____

_____

_____

_____

_____

_____

_____

_____

A. Direct Experience
B. Overcoming fears,
   night life
C. Dusk to night/
   anywhere
D. 1 or more
E. 4 years and up
F. Flashlight (optional)

The
Night

Barking coyotes, scratching noises, ghostly owl calls—strange sounds at night deepen the mystery of the unknown world of the outdoors.

Many of the animals that can be heard at night are seldom seen—owls and coyotes, for example. To increase your chances of spotting them, bring a flashlight to scan open clearings for their "eye shine." Hold the flashlight near your eyes (on your forehead or nose). If you want to see them without having them see you, put a red filter or a piece of red cellophane over your flashlight lens, since animals can't see red light.

World

Night hiking has other benefits besides the attraction of seeing nocturnal animals. Children are more reflective and communicative at night. I've noticed that as night falls a group of children will draw closer together for mutual support. After listening to the night sounds for a while, their conversation begins to turn to fears of the dark and of wild animals. Many times, discussion of their fears helps release them, and leaves everyone feeling relaxed and confident as we head back toward camp.

Survival Hike

"*If I got lost out here, how would I stay alive?*" Everyone who has hiked in wild places has imagined himself lost and alone, without gear or food. What would your chances of survival be, if it was just you and wilderness? To answer this question, take stock of how well you actually know the outdoors. Surviving in the wild is primarily a matter of familiarity with nature, and of taking care of ourselves by making intelligent use of what nature provides. The American Indian was able to live close to nature for countless centuries because he *knew* nature. He never dreaded being alone with the elements, but positively enjoyed the experience.

Knowing the skills of survival gives us a confidence and ease that help us to feel the innate bonds between ourselves and the world.

Survival outings can be lots of fun. They contain a built-in element of adventure, even when they last for only a few hours. As you become more and more skilled, you may want to test your abilities by going out for several days or a week at a time.

A good project for the initial outing is to learn how to construct a shelter from natural materials. Fort-building is a passion of childhood, and the surprising ingenuity and industry that children display can easily be tapped with the help of your informed suggestions.

The site of the shelter is important. If you build carelessly, you may find that what you thought was a cozy little hollow is actually a creek bed, when sudden rains bring a stream of water flowing cheerily through your front

A. Awaken Enthusiasm
B. Living with nature
C. Day and night/
   anywhere
D. 1 or more
E. 9 years and up
F. Basic equipment

room. Here are some suggestions for building a dry, comfortable lodge:

1) Build the shelter where it will receive the early morning sun (dawn is the coldest part of the day), and where it will be shaded from the hot afternoon sun in summer. 2) Avoid building your shelter under a canopy of evergreen leaves, as they will drip for hours after a snow or rainstorm. Avoid also building under dead trees, because they may drop a branch or two during a storm. 3) Build close to water and fuel (e.g., wood, or animal dung). 4) Find a breezy area, where there will be fewer mosquitoes in summer. 5) Don't build in a dry stream bed. 6) Make the shelter, or some ground signal that you've constructed, easily visible to searchers.

Be sure to use only dead materials in your practice sessions: there's no good excuse for desecrating the landscape except in an emergency.

Themes for subsequent hikes could be: finding water and fuel; building and lighting fires; finding and prepar-ing wild food; making equipment from natural materi-als, building various types of shelter; signaling for help; staying calm and quieting your fears when lost. You'll find much helpful discussion of these subjects in two survival source books: *Surviving the Unexpected Wilderness Emergency* by Gene Fear, published by and available from The Survival Education Association, Tacoma, WA; and *How to Stay Alive in the Woods* by Bradford Angier, pub-lished by Collier Books, New York, NY.

A. Share Inspiration
B. Fellowship, reflection
C. Day and night/ anywhere
D. Three or more
E. 10 years and up
F. Pencils & paper

AFTER A GROUP shares a deeply moving nature experience, I like to use the **Folding Poem** activity because it helps everyone express the inspiration they're feeling. It's a great way to end a week at camp, a memorable hike, or **Silent Sharing Walk** (see page 156). This activity was originally created by the North Carolina Outward Bound School.*

To begin, tell everyone that they'll be dividing up into teams of three, and each team will write a poem on the theme you've selected (some shared experience). Each person will have only partial knowledge of what else has been written.

The first person for each team writes the first line of the poem then passes it to the second person. This person writes one line that responds to the first writer's line, then writes another; then folds the poem so the third person sees only the last line written. The third person writes a line responding to the second person's last line, then writes another; then folds the poem so that the first writer sees only the last line. The first person writes the last line of the stanza. Below is a diagram of how it works.

LINES

| 1 | First Person | Writes a line |
| 2 | Second Person | Responds |

―――――――――――― fold ――――――――――――

(Second person folds here before...)

| 3 | Second Person | Writes a new line |
| 4 | Third Person | Responds |

―――――――――――― fold ――――――――――――

(Third person folds here before...)

| 5 | Third Person | Writes a new line |
| 6 | First Person | Responds |

* *EarthBook*, by Larry Crenshaw and the North Carolina Outward Bound School, Menasha Ridge Press, 3169 Cahaba Heights Road, Birmingham, AL, 35243, p. 116.

Now divide up into teams and pass out a pencil and paper to each team. Then tell the teams they have 10 to 15 minutes to write their poems. Teams can write more than six lines if they finish early. After all the teams have written their poems, have each team read theirs to the group. You'll be amazed at the beautiful continuity of thought that runs through the poems. You can also create poems that are written by everyone in the group by extending the same format above.

Below is an example of a **Folding Poem**. It was written by Ashleigh, Keith, and Paul at the Aigas Field Centre in Scotland after doing the **Tree Imagery** activity (from the sequel to this book, *Sharing the Joy of Nature*):

Folding Poem

Anchored deep within the Earth
Reaching high towards the clouds

Spreading green wings to catch the winds
Tiny seeds float away to settle in the deep moist Earth

Reaching down and up and out
The forest clothes the hills

Expanding

A. Direct Experience
B. Expansion of consciousness
C. Day and night/anywhere
D. One
E. 10 years and up
F. None

ALL OF US experience an expanded sense of freedom at times—when our awareness reaches out beyond ourselves and embraces the world around us. At such times, our spirits rise with the soaring vulture tilting and swaying high above. The wind may seem to breathe life into every passing tree; a frightened covey of quail explodes in flight, leaving our bodies trembling with a nervous thrill; or the steady roar of a swollen mountain stream, tumbling through a gorge far below, calms us and takes our thoughts high over the mountains into the unknown.

John Muir would sometimes become so engrossed in his wanderings in the Sierras that a one-day outing would become a trek lasting several days or even weeks. And in his travels he had none of the "essential" supplies like food, warm clothing, or even sleeping blankets. He was sustained by his love of beauty and solitude. Listen to his description of the inspiration that nourished him in wild places:

> *"Walk away quietly in any direction and taste the freedom of the mountaineer. . . . Climb the mountains and get their good tidings. Nature's peace will flow into you as sunshine flows into trees. The winds will blow their own freshness into you, and the storms their energies, while cares will drop off like autumn leaves."*

I have come to realize that when, like John Muir, we enter the world of nature in a spirit of openness, splendid experiences come to us unsought. Receptivity, along with our efforts to help and share with others, allows these inspirations to flow freely in our lives.

A special activity

Silent
Sharing
Walk

O F ALL THE ACTIVITIES in this book, the **Silent Sharing Walk** is potentially the most powerful. Walk in silence, abandoning words and the trappings of civilization—shoes, for example, and synthetic clothing that makes such un-nature-like noises. The silence and harmony of this activity, especially at dawn or dusk, create an awareness that we are sharing the world with all living things.

Animals can sense the state of mind of a group of humans; they won't run away if they feel a peaceful, harmonious intent. (Deer seem especially sensitive in this way.) Often I've noticed, on these walks, how animals will move away from us without the frantic fear so common at the approach of human beings; instead, they retreat a few steps at a time, stopping to look over their shoulders and satisfy their curiosity. It's wonderful to sense our kinship with animals; we enter their world as co-members, rather than as outsiders, and nature accepts us as part of itself.

Because the walk requires sensitivity and subtle appreciation, I offer it only to children who I feel will be receptive and able to enter into the spirit of silent sharing.

In a high forest in Southern California, twelve boys and I prepared for a **Silent Sharing Walk** by remaining alone and apart for a half-hour, in total silence. We then walked slowly down an old road that was overgrown and shaded by trees, toward an overlook where we would see the great Mojave Desert, stretching out and away, far below. Birds and insects sang a chorus, and the air seemed electrified by our silence. A boy would spot something and tap the shoulders of his companions, pointing to whatever had caught his attention. The boys' eyes testified to feelings of calmness and joy.

We saw a doe moving slowly toward us, intent on browsing in the roadside brush. When we were just 30 feet away, she gracefully raised her head and looked us over quietly. Her eyes were so innocent and trusting that they melted our hearts; rarely had we been accepted so unquestioningly into nature as now, by this gentle representative. There was an indescribable feeling about the moment—like coming home after a long exile.

Ten minutes later we came upon three coyotes trotting alongside the road. Like puppies, they would run a few feet closer, then stop to howl and tilt their heads from side to side as they watched us, curious about the silent strangers.

We arrived at the ledge overlooking the desert and stayed there for an hour, still in silence, letting ourselves be absorbed into the darkening high-desert world.

When a person becomes harmoniously attuned with the world, feelings of harmony with other people are intensified, too. Through watching nature in silence, we discover within ourselves feelings of relatedness with whatever we see—plants, animals, stones, Earth and sky. The American Indians knew that, in silence, we can feel that all things are expressions of a single Life, and that we humans, too, are children of that Life.

"As above, so below. As within, so without." As we get closer to nature, we find that the subject of our study is not actually nature at all, but life, and the nature of our own selves.

Unendingly magnificent is Nature; yet we view only one of Her billions of planets. Her splendor is spread across endless space and manifested on countless worlds; but, for us, Her most wondrous gift remains Her willingness to teach us about ourselves. And when we learn to see and understand ourselves and the world around us, we humans become the pinnacle of Nature's accomplishments; for through man, Nature is able to view and appreciate herself in the fullest, most vividly aware way of all.

Appendix

Clues for *Noses* and *Animal Game*

1. I move quickly now, but not so in my youth.
2. I usually hunt near water, but not always.
3. I eat flying insects.
4. I'm a strong flier.
5. Sometimes I'm very colorful.
6. I'm cold-blooded and I wear my skeleton on the outside instead of the inside.
7. I have two more legs than a mouse and have very large, compound eyes.
8. With my four wings I look like a helicopter flying in the air.

C Q Z F N M   E K X

1. My kind live in all of these places: lakes, marshes, salt bays, and beaches.
2. I have a long neck and a robust body; my sexes are alike in color.
3. My diet consists of mostly fish and crustaceans.
4. I nest on the ground in colonies.
5. My kind fly in orderly lines, and alternate several flaps with a glide. I can catch fish only by swimming.
6. I fly with my head hunched back on my shoulders.
7. I am a huge water bird with an 8 to 9 foot wing-span.
8. My great throat-pouches are handy for scooping up fish.
9. My close cousins (we've the same last name) live only by the ocean, while my species ventures more inland. I'm sure you'll be happy to know that my cousins are making a comeback from the DDT poisoning that depleted their numbers a few years ago.

V G H S D   O D K H B Z M

1. I will eat anything that moves and can be swallowed.
2. I hibernate in winter, except where it is warm.
3. I must live in damp or wet places, avoiding the dry heat of summer and the cold of winter.
4. Almost all of my kin lay their eggs in water.
5. I'm chunky and wouldn't win very many races.
6. Almost all my kin sing.
7. I can secrete a sticky white poison. In some of my kin this poison can kill or paralyze dogs and other predators who might try to eat them.
8. My close kin travel farther away from water than our distant cousins whom you might be thinking of. Also, it isn't true, as some say, that I will give you warts.

S N Z C

1. My body temperature is usually seven degrees warmer than man's.
2. Each foot of mine has two toes in front and two in back.
3. I usually undulate when I fly.
4. My stiff spiny tail feathers act as a prop when I hunt for my food.
5. My diet consists mainly of tree-boring insects, but also of ants, acorns, flying insects, berries, and sap.
6. My nest is a cavity in a tree that I make myself.
7. My bill is used for chiseling wood. With my long tongue I can catch insects living in a tree.

V N N C O D B J D Q

1. My sight is poor, but I can hear and smell very well.
2. My tail is six inches long or less.
3. I live mostly on forest floors and in thickets.
4. Both young and old of my kind are good climbers and when disturbed find safety in a tree.
5. My diet includes the following: small mammals, insects, and flesh, garbage, grasses, leaves, fruit, berries, and nuts.
6. When it starts to get cold and snows, I go inside for the winter.
7. I'm dark-colored, and sometimes weigh as much as five hundred pounds.

A D Z Q

1. I can walk and swim.
2. My vision is good, but I don't have a good sense of smell.
3. I care for and raise my young.
4. My body temperature stays the same.
5. My kind are very adaptable and live in many different environments.
6. I like to change my environment.
7. I walk on two feet and speak several different languages.

G T L Z M

1. During extreme hot and cold weather my home is also a home for many different kinds of animals.
2. I have small eyes and ears in relation to the rest of my body.
3. My front teeth are constantly growing.
4. I can run forward and backward.
5. My work is considered beneficial by humans if it is done out in the wilds.
6. I eat roots, stems, and leaves.
7. My heavily-built forefeet and long claws equip me for digging.
8. Look for mounds of dirt if you want to see where I've been working. My work is helpful because it tills the soil and allows more water to sink into the ground.
9. I see better than my neighbor the mole.

F N O G D Q

1. I feed my young milk, and lick their fur.
2. I'm sturdily built, but agile.
3. I'm more afraid of dogs than I am of humans.
4. My varied diet includes rodents, rabbits, birds, eggs, frogs, fish, insects, acorns, fruit, melons, carrion, and grain.
5. My home is a tree, rock pile, or large burrow.
6. I'm active at night.
7. My fingers are clever and curious.

8. I prefer to live mostly near streams and lakes.
9. The black mask over my eyes disguises me as I go out on my food raids. I usually like to wash any food I get before I eat it.

QZBBNNM

1. If you want to find me, look for water.
2. I'm a carnivore and eat mostly insects, and the smaller of my kind.
3. I am a fast, strong swimmer.
4. I need cold, well-oxygenated water to live in.
5. I spawn my eggs during the spring, in small clear streams.
6. I'm slim and sleek. I have scales and fins.
7. I'm as pretty as a rainbow.

QZHMANV SQNTS

Credits

Artwork:
Elizabeth Ann Kelley—Endpapers, 43, 54, 60-61, 62-63, 65, 72-73, 75, 76-77, 89, 106, 110-111, 117, 122-123, 134, 146-147, 160-161, 164-165
Dharani Das—100

Photographs:
John Hendrickson—Cover, Back Cover, 24, 27, 36, 43, 66, 98, 102, 120, 126, 136, 140, 142-143
Joseph Cornell—23, 40-41, 58-59, 91, 105, 119
Robert Frutos—3, 30, 71, 79, 82, 83, 92-93, 108, 124, 134, 173
Raghunath Polden—154-155, 158
Sue Landor—50-51
Lisa Yount—35
Rodney Polden—45
Judy Daniel—49
Larry Hierman—115
Colin Campbell—28
Roy Michel—52
Calif. Academy of the Sciences—112
David Simons—152
Unknown—12, 166
Sri Rama Publishing—18

First and Second Edition Design: Joshua M. Gitomer
Computer Production and Graphics: Rob Froelick
First Edition Composition: Dwan Typography

Acknowledgments

THIS BOOK, like an oak tree, has drawn nourishment from many sources. I would particularly like to thank these friends who, by their suggestions, encouragement, and support helped make this book possible.

James Fuller. A professional youth leader, he first suggested writing this book, and has lent his continued support to the project.

Kathe Goria, John Hendrickson, Dick Paterson. Many ideas and inspirations in this book came from years of fruitful associations with these friends and naturalists.

Garth Gilchrist. Much of Garth is contained within these pages. I am indebted to him also for a arranging a secluded and inspiring three-week stay on a houseboat in the Klamath Marsh, during which we were able to work without distractions—except for sightings of uncommon birds and mammals.

Michael Deranja, Nancy Graeber, Jean Rodgers, Joseph Selbie, Asha Praver, Kirtani Stickney, and my other friends at the Ananda Community, for their helpful expertise.

George Beinhorn, for his wonderful way with words, and *Josh Gitomer* and *Elizabeth Ann Kelley,* for bringing this book to life through their wonderful artwork and design.

Anandi Cornell, for her wisdom and clarity.

Alta Cal Audubon Chapter. Their generous financial support made the first printing of this book possible.

Indices

Attitudes & Qualities

Aesthetic Appreciation:

Bird Calling-114, Birds on a Stick-118, Earth Windows-22, Expanding-152, Sunset Watch-142, Tree Silhouettes-82, Vertical Poem-132.
(See also: Sensory Awareness.)

Assimilating New Facts:

Animal Clue Relay-92, Animal Game-72, Noses-70, What Animal Am I?-75, Wild Animal Scramble-86.

Concentration:

Bat and Moth-108, Blind Games-26, Duplication-48, Recon-Hike-122.

Empathy:

Birds on a Stick-118, Earth windows-22, Expanding-152, Find Your Age-80, Heartbeat in a Tree-25, Meet a Tree-28, Recipe for a Forest-58, Role-Playing-33, Sharing Your Site-134.

Fears (overcoming):

Being alone: Still Hunting-140.
Bugs: Earth windows-22, Micro-Hike-50.
Darkness: Camouflage-102, The Night World-146, Sunset Watch-142.
Wild animals: Calling Predators-120.

Imagination:

Blind Trail-30, Blind Walk-27, Caterpillar Walk-46, Earth Windows-22, Meet a Tree-28, Role-Playing-33.

Memory:

Animal Clue Relay-92, Animal Game-72, Duplication-48, Noses-70.

Merging With Nature:

Individual: Expanding-152, Still Hunting-140.
Group: Silent Sharing Walk-154.

Mixers:

Animal Game-72, Animal Parts-90, Noah's Ark-89, Pyramid of Life-52, Wild Animal Scramble-78.

Silence and Solitude (learning to enjoy them):

Blind Trail-30, Blind Walk-27, Earth Windows-22, Expanding-152, Sounds-40, Silent Sharing Walk-154, Still Hunting-140, Sunset Watch-142.

Social Reinforcement (of ecological attitudes):

Folding Poem-150, Sharing Your Site-134, Silent Sharing Walk-154.

Teamwork:

Animal Clue Relay-92, Animal Game-72, Animal Parts-90, Catch the Horse-100, Silent Sharing Walk-154.

Trust:

Blind Trail-30, Blind Walk-27.

Concepts

Physiology: Find Your Age-80, Heartbeat of a Tree-24, Plant Succession Crawl-64.

Silhouettes: Tree Silhouettes-82.

Review:

Owls and Crows-78.

Sensory Awareness:

All senses except visual: Back Home-47, Blind Trail-30, Blind Walk-27, Caterpillar Walk-46. *Auditory:* Bat and Moth-108, Sounds-40.

Tactile: Meet a Tree-28.

Visual: Colors-41, Duplication-48, Earth Windows-22, Unnature Trail-42.

All (except taste): Adventure Hunt-131.

Stalking:

Sleeping Miser-106, Recon-Hike-122.

Environment

Almost Anywhere:

Animal Clue Relay-92, Animal Game-72, Animal Parts-90, Bat and Moth-108, Blind Walk-27, Calling Predators-120, Caterpillar Walk-46, Colors-41, Duplication-48, Expanding-152, Identification Game-76, Noah's Ark-89, Noses-70, Owls and Crows-78, Predator-Prey-62, Pyramid of Life-54, Role-Playing-33, Scavenger Hunt-84, Sleeping Miser-106, Sounds-40, Unnature Trail-42, Vertical Poem-132, Webbing-60, What Animal Am I?-75, Wild Animal Scramble-86.

Forest:

Bird Calling-114, Birds on a Stick-118, Blind Trail-30, Earth Windows-22, Find Your Age-80, Heartbeat of a Tree-24, Meet a Tree-28, Recipe for a Forest-58, Silent Sharing Walk-154, Still Hunting-140, Survival Hike-148, Tree Silhouettes-82.

Indoors:

Animal Clue Relay-92, Animal Game-72, Animal Parts-90, Bat and Moth-108, Folding Poem-150, Identification Game-76, Noah's Ark-89, Noses-70, Owls and Crows-78, Predator-Prey-62, Pyramid of Life-54, Recipe for a Forest-58, Role-Playing-33, Tree Silhouettes-82, Vertical Poem-132, Webbing-60, What Animal Am I?-75, Wild Animal Scramble-86.

Meadow:

All Awaken Enthusiasm games, Catch the Horse-100, Micro-Hike-50.

Natural Area (with variety of habitats):

Adventure Hunt-131, Sharing Your Site-134, Journey to the Heart of Nature activities-126.

Evening:

Sunset Watch-142.

Night:

    Camouflage-102, The Night World-146, Watcher of the Road-110.

Pond:

    Plant Succession Crawl-64.

Thicket:

    Bird Calling-114, Birds on a Stick-118, Calling Predators-120, Still Hunting-140.

Viewpoint:

    Sunset Watch-142.

Mood (G = suitable for group only)

Energetic/Playful: Otter

    Animal Clue Relay (G)-92, Animal Game (G)-72, Animal Parts (G)-90, Bat and Moth (G)-108, Catch the Horse (G)-100, Identification Game (G)-76, Noah's Ark (G)-89, Noses-70, Owls and Crows (G)-78, Predator-Prey (G)-62, Pyramid of Life (G)-54, Webbing (G)-60, What Animal Am I? (G)-75, Wild Animal Scramble (G)-86, Wildmen in the Alders (G)-104.

Attentive/Observational: Crow

    Adventure Hunt-131, Camouflage (G)-102, Caterpillar Walk (G)-46, Colors-41, Duplication-48, Find Your Age-80, Micro-Hike-50, Plant Succession Crawl-64, Recon-Hike-122, Scavenger Hunt (G)-84, Sleeping Miser (G)-106, Sounds-40, Survival Hike-148, Tree Silhouettes-82, Unnature Trail-42, Watcher of the Road (G)-110.

Calm/Experiential: Bear

    Back Home-47, Bird Calling-114, Birds on a Stick-118, Blind Trail-30, Blind Walk-27, Calling Predators-120, Earth Windows-22, Expanding-152, Heartbeat of a Tree-24, Meet a Tree-28, The Night World-146, Role-Playing-33, Still Hunting-140, Sunset Watch-142, Vertical Poem-132.

Reflective/Sharing: Dolphin

    Folding Poem (G)-150, Recipe for a Forest-58, Sharing Your Site-134, Silent Sharing Walk-154.

Sharing Nature Foundation
Sharing Nature Worldwide

JOSEPH CORNELL and other teachers personally trained by him offer nature awareness workshops throughout the year through the Sharing Nature Foundation. These programs are based on Mr. Cornell's years of experience teaching nature awareness. They draw extensively on the activities and philosophy presented in the four-volume Sharing Nature Series: *Sharing Nature with Children, Sharing the Joy of Nature, Journey to the Heart of Nature,* and *Listening to Nature.*

Every summer Joseph Cornell also conducts a week-long conference retreat in Assisi, Italy or Northern California. Participants experience many ways of deepening their enjoyment of the natural world and come away with effective and inspirational tools they can use both professionally and personally.

In addition, Sharing Nature Worldwide is an international association of organizations and individuals using Cornell's philosophy and activities.

To find out more about Sharing Nature coordinators and programs in other countries, foreign translations of Cornell's books, and his schedule and workshops, please visit the Sharing Nature web site at **http://www.sharingnature.com.** To sponsor a program, or to find out more about the summer conference, write or call the Sharing Nature Foundation at 14618 Tyler Foote Road, Nevada City, CA 95959; or telephone or fax: (530) 478-7650.

Education for Life
Ananda Schools
& Communities

FOR MANY YEARS Joseph Cornell has been associated with the Education for Life Foundation and Ananda Schools which, since 1972, have taught young people through a balanced program of physical, mental, emotional and spiritual training. In addition to excellence in academics, the curriculum includes those living skills that will enable children to experience true success in life—how to get along with others, how to live in harmony with the Earth, how to concentrate, and how to achieve and maintain inner peace, among other skills. Six broad curriculum areas include self-expression and communication, understanding people, our Earth/ our universe, personal development, cooperation, and wholeness.

To know more about the educational philosophy that has inspired Mr. Cornell's writings and teaching, you may wish to read *Education for Life* by J. Donald Walters (Crystal Clarity, Publishers). To learn more about the Education for Life philosophy, Ananda School campus sites, and teacher training programs write or call Ananda School at 14618 Tyler Foote Road, Nevada City, CA 95959, (530) 478-7640 or visit the Education for Life web site at **http://www.efl.org.**

Since 1975 Mr. Cornell has been a resident of Ananda World Brotherhood Village, a highly successful intentional community based on the teachings of Paramhansa Yogananda (author of *Autobiography of a Yogi*). Today there are sister Ananda communities in the United States, Europe, Australia, and Africa. If you would like to know more about these communities write to Ananda Village at the above address, or visit the web site at **http://www.ananda.org.**

About the Author

FROM HIS EARLIEST YEARS, Joseph Cornell has felt a sensitive attunement with the mysteries and beauties of nature. As a boy, he spent much time exploring the marshes, orchards, and mountains near his home in northern California.

Cornell has spent most of his adult life outdoors, too, showing others the wonders of nature. Joseph designed his own Bachelor of Science degree program in nature awareness at California State University in Chico. He received formal training as a naturalist with the National Audubon Society. Then, for seven years, he taught in public school outdoor education programs, and as a naturalist for the Boy Scouts of America. In 1979, he established the Sharing Nature Foundation to share his methods and philosophy with adults and teachers.

Today, as one of the world's leading nature educators, Cornell's workshops on nature awareness have been attended by tens of thousands of people around the globe. *Sharing Nature with Children,* the first in the Sharing Nature Series, has sold over 450,000 copies and has been translated into more than fifteen languages.

The Sharing Nature Series
by Joseph Cornell

Volume One:
Sharing Nature with Children
The Classic Parents' and Teachers'
Nature Awareness Guidebook

Volume Two:
Sharing the Joy of Nature
The Handbook for Nature Teachers
with Nature Activities for All Ages
A sequel to Volume One, a treasury of games for all ages, plus a practical handbook for nature educators in which Cornell explains the Flow Learning teaching method.

Volume Three:
Journey to the Heart of Nature
A Guided Exploration, especially for Young Adults
Through stories, activities and extended visits to a self-chosen special place in nature, Cornell conducts the reader to an ever-deepening appreciation of that place—and for all natural places.

Volume Four:
Listening to Nature
A Journey of Beauty into the Essence of Nature
A now-classic book for meditative and dynamic ways of achieving peace through nature—yet light, with stunning photographs and full of Cornell's irrepressible enthusiasm.

Sharing the Joy of Nature Video
Filmed in the high Sierras, Cornell shares his nature awareness teaching techniques as well as his exuberance in this beautiful 40-minute video.

Activity Masters
[see p. 135]

A Sharing Nature Walk Audio Cassette
[see p. 117]

Available from Dawn Publications
800-545-7475

Other distinctive Nature Awareness titles from Dawn Publications

Play Lightly on the Earth, by Jacqueline Horsfall. Written especially with 3 to 9 year olds in mind, *Play Lightly* is packed with original activities developed by the author over her 15 years as a nature educator. They are based on sound scientific concepts with an emphasis on creative thinking, problem-solving, and skill development—all in the guise of play. Fifty activities, 176 pages. Endorsed by Joseph Cornell.

The Dandelion Seed, by Joseph Anthony, follows a seed through a lifelong journey filled with exploration, challenges and fulfillment, a metaphor for us all.

Places of Power, by Michael DeMunn, reveals the places of power that native people all over the world have always known, and how to let your place of power speak to your open heart.

The Tree in the Ancient Forest, by Carol Reed-Jones, reveals in cumulative verse the remarkable interdependent web of plants and animals living around a single old fir tree.

A Swim through the Sea, A Walk in the Rainforest, and **A Fly in the Sky,** a trilogy by Kristin Joy Pratt, are three joyful, illustrated tours of some of Earth's most important biospheres.

Teachers: ask about our **Sharing Nature With Children Series** of teacher's guides by Bruce and Carol Malnor—a practical and creative way to incorporate Dawn's books into the school curriculum. Ask also for information about school visits by our authors and illustrators.

Dawn Publications is dedicated to inspiring in children a deeper understanding and appreciation for all life on Earth. For a copy of our catalog please call 800-545-7475.

Please also visit our web site at **www.dawnpub.com.**